NEW YORK WILDLIFE VIEWING GUIDE

Frank Knight, Author
Markly Wilson, Project Manager
Illustrations by Jean Gawalt

FALCON®

HELENA, MONTANA

Design, typesetting, and other prepress work by Falcon® Publishing,
Helena, Montana. Printed in Korea.

Library of Congress Cataloging-in-Publication Data

Knight, Frank, 1936–
    New York wildlife viewing guide / Frank Knight.
        p.   cm.
    ISBN 1-56044-513-0 (paperback)
    1. Wildlife viewing sites—New York—Guidebooks. 2. Wildlife
watching—New York—Guidebooks. 3. New York—Guidebooks.
I. Title.
QL 195.K55   1998
599' .09747—dc   97-4430
                                                              CIP

Front cover photo
Gray squirrel: Breck P. Kent

Back cover photos
Hudson River and Iona Island from Bear Mountain: Hardie Truesdale
Red fox: Herb Segars

New York State Project Manager
Markly Wilson

Author
Frank Knight

National Wildlife Viewing Guide Program Manager
Kate Davies, Defenders of Wildlife

Illustrations
Jean Gawalt

CONTENTS

ACKNOWLEDGMENTS

The *New York Wildlife Viewing Guide* is the result of more than four years of collaboration by many individuals and organizations dedicated to sustaining and sharing the enjoyment of New York's diverse wildlife and its habitats.

The committee members guiding the project (some of whom have since changed positions) have been: Jean Gawalt and Frank Knight, NYS Department of Environmental Conservation; Alane Ball, The Nature Conservancy; James Berg, NYS Council of Chambers of Commerce; Alexander Brash, New York City Parks and Recreation; Gordon Colvin, NYSDEC; Graham Cox, Empire State Development; Clay Grove, USDA Forest Service; Ann Harrison, NYS Office of Parks, Recreation and Historic Preservation; Berna Lincoln, Federation of NYS Bird Clubs; Andrew Mason, Audubon Council of New York State; Michael Matthews, NYSDEC; David Miller, N.Y. Trappers Association; Debbie Nelson and Kurt Weiskotten, NYS Department of Transportation; Karl Parker, NYS DEC; Peter Roemer, American Wildlife Research Foundation, David Taft and John Tanacredi, National Park Service; Tom Elliot, New York State Museum; Don V. Tiller, US Fish and Wildlife Service; Michael Urban, NYSDEC; and Dr. Stephen Zawistowski of New York ASPCA.

Special gratitude is due to Jean Gawalt for his invaluable dedication to this project and his persistence from the very beginning; to Alexander Brash, whose Manhattan perspective added valuable quality to the project; to Doris Herwig for her wisdom and behind-the-scenes work; to Peg Chagnon, who contributed countless hours of computer expertise and her meticulous attention to detail; to Frances Steans, whose secretarial skills helped maintain order; Paul Zank of the DEC for his enthusiastic guidance; to Andrew Mason, Audubon Council of New York State for his constant support; and to Frank Knight, who authored the guide.

The success of the project is also due to the vision and support of decision makers who clearly demonstrated their appreciation of the value of this program to New York. These include Gary Parsons, Chief Wildlife Biologist, NYSDEC; Ed Martin, Executive Deputy Commissioner; Linda Wohlers, Deputy Commissioner, Advertising Marketing and Tourism of Empire State Development, Division of Tourism; and Kate Davies of Defenders of Wildlife.

We are also grateful for the work of numerous site and agency employees and volunteers who participated in the site-nomination and information-gathering processes. Many places to see wildlife across the state are not included; subsequent guides will reveal even more.

PROJECT SPONSORS

 The NEW YORK STATE DEPARTMENT OF ENVIRONMEN-
TAL CONSERVATION (DEC) has two main functions: natural
resource management and environmental quality protection.

It is the DEC's responsibility to protect, improve, and conserve the state's land, waters, air, fish, wildlife, and other resources in order to enhance the health, safety, and welfare of the people of the
state and their overall economic and social well being.

During the last quarter century, New Yorkers have witnessed a remarkable
recovery of the state's waters, air, and land; a renewal of fish, wildlife, and forest resources; an expansion of accessible recreation, and the development of
safe waste management. Today, in the spirit of equal and cooperative environmental responsibilities, Governor Pataki is helping government, business, and
individuals forge partnerships that protect and enhance the state's natural
resources while nurturing a healthy business climate.

 DEFENDERS OF WILDLIFE is a national nonprofit organization of more than 200,000 members and supporters dedicated
to preserving the natural abundance and diversity of wildlife
and its habitat. A one-year membership is $20 and includes a
subscription to *Defenders*, an award-winning conservation
magazine. To join, or for further information, write or call Defenders of Wildlife, 1101 Fourteenth Street NW, Washington, DC 20005; 202-682-9400. Visit
their web site at http://www.defenders.org.

 The NEW YORK STATE DEPARTMENT OF TRANSPORTA-
TION strives to ensure that the traveling public has a safe, effi-
cient, and environmentally sound multi-modal transportation
system. Through a network of 115,000 miles of highway and
4,600 miles of railroad, residents and visitors alike are able to
enjoy the vast natural splendor found throughout the state. The department
publishes an official highway map, which is available free of charge at visitor
centers. The NYSDOT headquarters is located at 1220 Washington Ave.,
Albany, NY 12232-0524; 518-457-6400.

 THE AMERICAN SOCIETY FOR THE PREVENTION OF
CRUELTY TO ANIMALS was established by Henry Bergh in
1866 "to provide effective means for the prevention of cruelty
to animals." Through education, legislation, advocacy, shelters,
animal hospitals, and law enforcement, the ASPCA dedicates its
resources to increasing awareness, encouraging humane lifestyles, and elimi-
nating cruelty to animals. It is the oldest animal-protection organization in the
Western Hemisphere.

THE AUDUBON COUNCIL OF NEW YORK STATE, INC. is
composed of the 32 chapters of the National Audubon Society in the state. The Audubon Council and its member
chapters are dedicated to conserving and restoring natural
ecosystems—focusing on birds, other wildlife, and their

habitats—for the benefit of humanity and the earth's biological diversity. The council and local chapters engage in education, advocacy, and research in pursuit of these goals.

The following New York State Audubon chapters contributed significantly to this guide: Delaware-Otsego, Genesee Valley, Huntington, North Fork, Northern Catskills, Onondaga, Rockland, and South Shore.

The URBAN PARK RANGERS are the uniformed environmental educators of the City of New York Department of Parks and Recreation. Since 1979, the Urban Park Rangers have introduced school groups and the public to the 26,000 acres of park land in New York City. Through environmental and historical education, active conservation, and enforcement of rules and regulations, the Urban Park Rangers foster an ecologically healthy and safe park system. The rangers are pleased to support the Watchable Wildlife Program and to inform people about the rich and diverse natural wildlife habitats in New York City. For more information contact: Urban Park Rangers, Arsenal North, 1234 Fifth Avenue, New York, NY 10029; 212-360-2774.

The USDA FOREST SERVICE is responsible for managing National Forest lands and their resources, and for protecting and restoring these lands to best serve the needs of the American people. For more information, contact USDA Forest Service, Finger Lakes National Forest, 5218 State Route 414, Hector, NY 14841; 607-546-4470.

The U.S. FISH AND WILDLIFE SERVICE is pleased to support this project in furtherance of its mission to conserve, protect, and enhance fish and wildlife resources and their habitats. Additional funding for this project was provided through Partners for Wildlife, a federal aid grants program administered by the U.S. Fish and Wildlife Service. For further information, contact the U.S. Fish and Wildlife Service, 300 Westgate Center Drive, Hadley, MA 01035; 413-253-8200.

The DEPARTMENT OF DEFENSE is the steward of about 25 million acres of land in the United States, many of which contain irreplaceable natural and cultural resources. The DOD is pleased to support the National Watchable Wildlife Program through its Legacy Resource Management Program, a special initiative to enhance the conservation and restoration of natural and cultural resources on military land. For more information contact ODUSD (ES) EQ-LP, 3400 Defense Pentagon, Room 3E791, Arlington, VA 20301-3400.

State of New York
Executive Chamber
State Capitol
Albany 12224

Dear Friend:

New York State is world-famous for tourist attractions such as Niagara Falls, the Empire State Building, and the Baseball Hall of Fame. However, until now, another facet of our wealth of attractions has largely gone unnoticed. In addition to magnificent vistas and bountiful natural resources, New York State boasts an impressive variety of wildlife that you can view from your car and along hiking trails.

Whether it's white-tailed deer, wild turkey, foxes, or bald eagles, the *New York Wildlife Viewing Guide* makes it easy to find just the right spot for viewing our state's wildlife. Besides highlighting the 76 best places in New York to see wildlife in natural habitats, this informative guide will also help you plan your excursion. It has tips on the best travel times and things to bring along, as well as descriptions of your destinations and the sights you can expect to see.

The *New York Wildlife Viewing Guide* is the result of a partnership between the public and private sectors—state and federal agencies, nonprofit organizations, and New York businesses. On behalf of all those who have worked to bring you this guide, welcome to New York State! I hope you have an enjoyable visit and great wildlife viewing.

Very truly yours,

George E. Pataki

INTRODUCTION

From the surf and dunes of Long Island's seashore to the alpine-high peaks of the Adirondacks, New York's spectacular scenery attracts millions of human visitors while providing crucial habitat for plants and animals. This guide is designed to help you see and enjoy New York's plentiful wildlife.

And plentiful it is! New York's diverse habitats support more than 80 species of native mammals, from the tiniest shrew to bear, moose, and whales. Tens of thousands of insects, from the smallest springtails and vital honeybees to gorgeous moths and butterflies, fascinating in themselves, provide the food base for many larger animals, especially birds. More than 240 bird species, such as the bluebird and bald eagle, nest in New York each year, and almost another 200 pass through on their biannual migrations. Seventeen each of turtle and snake species, three lizards, 11 frogs, three toads, and 18 salamanders make up our reptile and amphibian species list. Hundreds of fish species make cold mountain streams, warm shallow ponds, deep lakes, tidal rivers, and pounding surf their home.

Residents and visitors can enjoy this bounty of wildlife at hundreds of private nonprofit and public-access sites across the state. We present only 76 of them here, with site descriptions, information on what to look for, and directions explaining how to get there. This guide will help you see more wildlife, but remember that it is possible that you will see very few—or even none—of the mentioned animals on any given trip. Wild animals' very survival often depends on their skill at not being seen. If you can take as much pleasure in the looking as in the seeing, your wildlife quests will always be successful adventures.

Ruddy turnstone feeding on a horseshoe crab, Long Island. TOM VEZO

You may want to seek additional help in seeing and identifying wildlife. Many of the staffed facilities in this guide, as well as local Audubon chapters, offer guided walks to see and identify birds, other animals, and plants. This guidance from more experienced wildlife watchers is a great help to beginners. You may also learn about other places known for their wildlife watching opportunities. The Nature Conservancy and other environmental organizations publish regional guides to natural areas. Since these special places are available for your enjoyment at very little or no cost to you, you may wish to support the public agencies and private organizations listed as partners in this guide that work to acquire and protect wildlife habitats.

THE NATIONAL WATCHABLE WILDLIFE PROGRAM

The National Watchable Wildlife Program is a nationwide cooperative effort to combine wildlife conservation with America's deepening interest in wildlife-related outdoor recreation. Since the 1970s, wildlife viewing has grown to be one of the most popular outdoor recreational activities.

For many years, hunters and anglers have supplied most of the funding for wildlife conservation by paying license fees and taxes on firearms and fishing tackle. These dollars funded public fish and wildlife areas, refuges, preserves, and management programs, all of which benefited wildlife—game and nongame animals alike. Though there is a long tradition of hunting in New York and the sport has remained strong here, national trends indicate that participation is dropping. This change has generated concern about the future source of funding for wildlife conservation and wildlife-related recreation. Efforts are underway at state and national levels to develop new funding mechanisms. The Watchable Wildlife Program was founded on the premise that people who enjoy and learn about wildlife in a natural setting will become advocates for conservation in the future.

The National Watchable Wildlife Program began in 1990 with the signing of a Memorandum of Understanding by eight federal land management agencies, the International Association of Fish and Wildlife Agencies, and four national conservation groups. Defenders of Wildlife assumed the role of national program coordinator. The cornerstone of this program is the series of state-by-state wildlife viewing guides. The *New York Wildlife Viewing Guide* is the 26th guide in this Watchable Wildlife series. The location of each of the sites mentioned in this book is marked with a sign bearing the brown-and-white binocular logo featured on the cover. Similar viewing networks with sites marked by this logo have been established in more than half of the 50 states.

The partnership formed to produce the New York guide and the accompanying viewing network will continue to work together on site development, site interpretation, and conservation education. Viewing sites will be enhanced with interpretive signs, trails, boardwalks, or viewing platforms. In addition, opportunities to participate in wildlife viewing programs will be available in the future.

Mammal diversity: *New York's diverse habitats provide food and living space for more than 80 species of native mammals, from the tiniest shrew to bear and moose. Some mammals, like the gray squirrel, are found nearly every-where. Others, like the Indiana bat, are listed as endangered species. Several, like the beaver and fisher, were nearly lost but have been restored by the Department of Environmental Conservation's Division of Fish and Wildlife's management practices.*

NEW YORK'S BIODIVERSITY

Biodiversity, the abbreviated way of referring to biological diversity, is a term that describes the great variety of living things. When we think of living things, we often think first of individual plants and animals, like a deer or an oak tree. We then extend this to include the populations of individual spe-cies—all of the deer in a herd or all of the oak trees in a forest. But diversity

Bird Diversity: *New York's diverse habitats also provide food and living space for more than 240 bird species that nest here each year. Nearly another 200 species pass through our state during annual migrations. Some, like the chickadee and blue jay, can be seen across the state year-round. Others, like the northern oriole and chimney swift, winter far to the south, where insect food abounds. Through the determined efforts of Department of Environmental Conservation wildlife personnel and hundreds of dedicated volunteers, several birds have been restored to healthier populations. Two of these are our state bird, the Eastern bluebird, and our national bird, the bald eagle.*

must also include the variety of habitats where populations live. A habitat is made up of all the populations of plants and animals and decomposers in any given area, as well as all of its non-living components—light, air, water, and soil.

New York's wildlife diversity is unequaled in the Northeast. This is true mainly because New York has larger and more types of natural habitats than

Reptile and Amphibian Diversity: *New York's diverse habitats provide homes for nearly 70 species of reptiles and amphibians. Our reptiles include 17 turtle species, 3 lizards and 17 snakes. Among New York amphibians are 11 species of frogs, 3 toads and 18 salamanders. No other group of animals presents as much of a challenge to the Division of Fish and Wildlife personnel responsible for animal protection. Forty percent of our reptiles and 22 percent of our amphibians are listed as endangered, threatened, or special concern species. Reptiles and amphibians are especially sensitive to the major causes of wildlife decline: habitat loss, pollution, and illegal collection.*

any of its neighbors. Larger and more diverse habitats result in more wildlife diversity. Ecologists have identified several hundred saltwater, tidal, freshwater, and terrestrial natural and human-altered habitats in New York State. From our Atlantic and Great Lakes shorelines to the alpine summits in the Adirondacks, New York's more than 49,000 square miles of land and water

Fish Diversity: *Cold mountain streams, warm shallow ponds, deep lakes, tidal rivers, and pounding surf are just some of the many diverse water bodies which support hundreds of fish species.*

offer residents and visitors some of America's most scenic natural settings and provide homes for hundreds of fish and wildlife species.

Beyond the enjoyment seeing wildlife provides, biodiversity benefits us in many ways. It provides a vast reservoir of materials for use in medicine, agriculture, and industry. Habitats with high diversity are healthier and more stable than those with fewer key components. For example, if an insect or disease temporarily causes a serious problem for a population of a specific plant, in a diverse ecosystem, some of the many other plants there can provide wildlife with pollen, nectar, food, or shelter until the harmed plant can recover. Biodiversity also provides us with so-called "ecological housekeeping" services. These include fruit and vegetable pollination, pest and flood control,

Insect Diversity: *New York's diverse wildlife habitats provide food and living space for tens of thousands of species of native and introduced insects. Our largest group of animals ranges in size from the tiniest springtails to large mantids, moths and butterflies. A great many of the animals pictured in these paintings depend either directly or indirectly on insects for much of their food, and are our best allies in controlling insect pest species. Many predacious insects help control other insects.*

and water and air purification—all at no cost to human society. In fact, the sun's energy, which makes our world work, is available to us only through the energy fixing, utilizing, and dispensing activities of plants and animals. If everyone understood this concept, we all would take better care that New York's diversity of habitats is protected now and into the future.

HOW TO USE THIS GUIDE

Wildlife species' presence and abundance in any part of the state are determined by topography, climate, soils, and natural vegetation. For that reason it makes sense to divide the state into wildlife-viewing ecozones rather than by political boundaries like counties or tourism regions. Biologists have divided New York into more than a dozen ecozones and sub-zones, however, we have simplified and consolidated these into seven ecozones for this publication: the Catskills, the Appalachian Plateau (the Southern Tier), the Great Lakes Plain (including the St. Lawrence River Valley), the Adirondacks, the Hudson and Mohawk valleys, New York City, and the Coastal Lowlands (Long Island). Each ecozone forms a chapter of this book.

Each site **description** includes the habitats where wildlife may be seen and amenities like trails, boardwalks, and observation towers to enhance your visit. **Viewing information** mentions wildlife species that are most likely to be encountered at a site. Icons display available facilities and recreational opportunities. Knowing the site's **owner** and phone number enables you to obtain additional site information. **Directions** to the site from major highways like the New York State Thruway help you find your way; use in conjunction with an ordinary roadmap. Each viewing site will eventually be marked by a binoculars logo, found at wildlife viewing sites across the nation.

FACILITIES AND RECREATION

| Entry or Use Fee | Parking | Restrooms | Barrier- Free | Restaurant | Picnic Area | Lodging | Camping |

| Hiking | Bicycling | Cross- Country Skiing | Horse Trails | Boat Ramp | Large Boats | Small Boats |

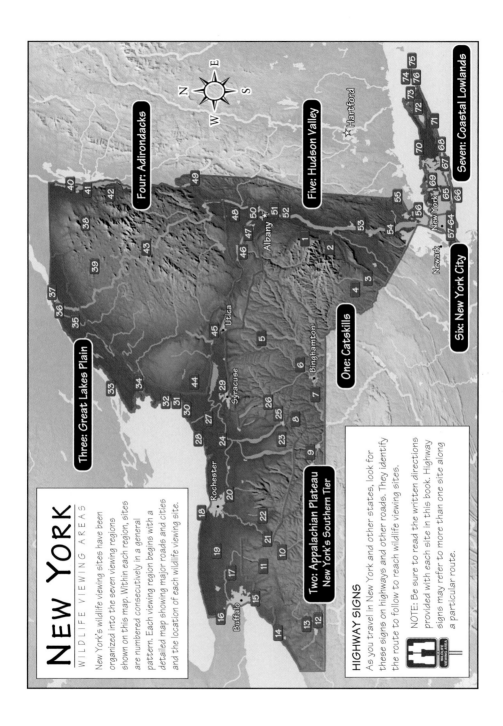

NEW YORK

WILDLIFE VIEWING AREAS

New York's wildlife viewing sites have been organized into the seven viewing regions shown on this map. Within each region, sites are numbered consecutively in a general pattern. Each viewing region begins with a detailed map showing major roads and cities and the location of each wildlife viewing site.

Three: Great Lakes Plain

Four: Adirondacks

Five: Hudson Valley

One: Catskills

Two: Appalachian Plateau
New York's Southern Tier

Six: New York City

Seven: Coastal Lowlands

HIGHWAY SIGNS

As you travel in New York and other states, look for these signs on highways and other roads. They identify the route to follow to reach wildlife viewing sites.

NOTE: Be sure to read the written directions provided with each site in this book. Highway signs may refer to more than one site along a particular route.

WILDLIFE VIEWING AREA

Cities: Buffalo, Rochester, Syracuse, Utica, Binghamton, Albany, Newark, New York, Hartford

VIEWING HINTS

• **The first and last daylight hours** are generally the best times to view or photograph animals. Wildlife viewing is usually poorest during the middle of the day.

• **Get familiar with wildlife species' behaviors and habitats.** Different times of the day and seasons of the year may find the same species in different habitats. For example, a hen wild turkey with a brood of young chicks may wander along a grassy woods road in early morning to avoid wet vegetation and to catch insects. Later in the day, at noon, they may be in a hot, sunny hayfield dusting in a bare patch. In the evening, you may see them along that same woods road, this time flying up into a roost tree, which they may use many nights in succession.

• **Be quiet and move slowly.** Noisy, quick movement normally scares wildlife. Use your car as an effective "blind" to view animals without alarming

Watching turtles at a beaver pond at Five Rivers Environmental Education Center, Delmar. THOMAS D. LINDSAY

them. Whenever cover is unavailable, sit quietly, act disinterested, and gaze all around; try not to stare directly at wildlife.

• **Binoculars, spotting scopes, and telephoto camera lenses** will help you see animals more closely. You are probably too close if animals alter their behavior, stop feeding, or appear nervous. If you note these signs, sit quietly or move slowly away until they resume their initial behavior.

• **Hats, sunglasses, sunscreen, and insect repellant** will enhance your viewing enjoyment. Extra clothing and rain gear prepare you for weather changes.

• **Be patient.** Wait quietly for animals to enter or return to an area. Give yourself plenty of time to allow animals to move within your view. Patience is often rewarded with a more complete viewing experience.

• **Use all your senses** when looking for wildlife, and think about what, where, and when wildlife will reveal itself to you.

• **Plan ahead** a little if time allows—note what species are likely to be found at a site you plan to visit. Then go to your library and learn a bit about those species. Often, knowing something about the animals ahead of time will help you immeasurably when you are afield. Animals are not just out there "striking a pose" and awaiting your visit, and your preparation can be as much fun as the field trip itself.

OUTDOOR ETHICS

• Honor the rights of private landowners and gain permission before entering their property.

• Respect the rights of other wildlife viewers. Approaching animals too closely, making loud noises, and sudden movements are inappropriate.

• Avoid feeding the animals—for their sake and for yours. Animals accustomed to being fed at roadsides are more likely to be hit by vehicles. The possibility of disease transmittal is also enhanced. Large animals like bears and even deer can become aggressive and dangerous if they become panhandlers.

• Neither people nor pets should ever chase wildlife, and harassment of wild animals is unlawful. Pets are best left at home during wildlife viewing excursions.

• Wild baby animals look cute and helpless, but resist the urge to handle young creatures. They usually have not been orphaned or abandoned; their parents are most likely nearby.

• Please do not handle dead wildlife nor traces like scat or pellets. Allow nature to do its recycling and keep yourself safe by avoiding potential contact with animal diseases, some of which are transmittable to people.

• Ensure your own right to enjoy the outdoors in the future. Leave wildlife habitat in better condition than you found it. Pick up any litter you find and dispose of it properly.

REGION ONE: CATSKILLS

Erosion-resistant, 400 million-year-old sandstone is responsible for this scenic treasure, now safeguarded as part of a "forever wild" State Forest Preserve. With elevations of more than 2,000 feet to peaks ranging from 3,000 to nearly 4,200 feet, the Catskills are home to wildlife found in the Adirondacks, notably black bear and Bicknell's thrush. An extensive hiking trail system encourages exploration of this wilderness area beyond the sites mentioned here.

Many of the trails are easy to climb and don't require special equipment or great physical stamina—where else can you go for a delightful three-hour hike and see warblers, hear wild turkey gobble, and find huge beech trees with

five-toed claw marks running the length of the trunk showing where a black bear has climbed and foraged? The Mongaup area, in the lower elevations of this zone, provides a premier place to see bald eagles in the winter, while the extensive wetlands of the Bashakill are home to dozens of species of birds and mammals.

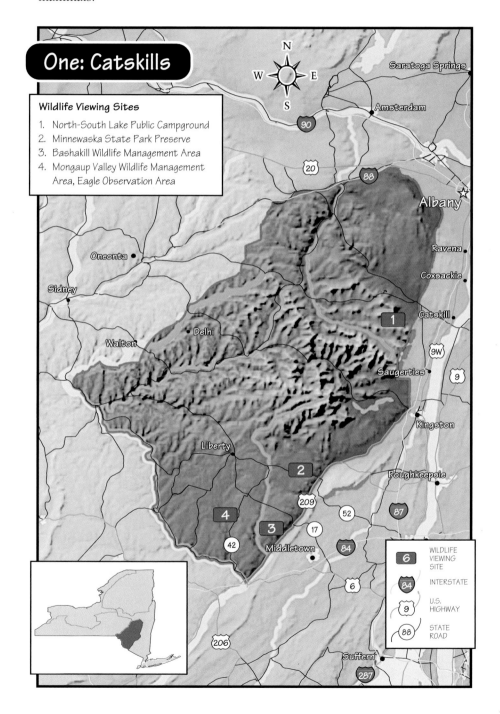

One: Catskills

Wildlife Viewing Sites

1. North-South Lake Public Campground
2. Minnewaska State Park Preserve
3. Bashakill Wildlife Management Area
4. Mongaup Valley Wildlife Management Area, Eagle Observation Area

6	WILDLIFE VIEWING SITE
84	INTERSTATE
9	U.S. HIGHWAY
88	STATE ROAD

1. NORTH-SOUTH LAKE PUBLIC CAMPGROUND

Description: The largest public campground in the Catskills, North-South Lake offers tent and trailer sites, two lakes, two beaches, rowboat and canoe rentals, fishing, picnic areas and pavilions, and a playing field. Numerous hiking trails provide easy access to wildlife viewing and incredible vistas. Near the site of the Catskill Mountain House, a former hotel, a trail enables hikers to enjoy the same picturesque scenes once enjoyed by the guests: Artist's Rock, Sunset Rock, Newman's Ledge, and Boulder Rock. Just outside the campground, reached from a trail beginning on Route 23A, is Kaaterskill Falls, the state's highest with tiers 250 and 260 feet high.

Viewing Information: North-South Lake provides opportunities to see a good cross-section of wildlife common to the Catskills. White-tailed deer and signs of black bear are common and the black bear themselves are also sometimes seen. Wild turkey and ruffed grouse frequent the woods, as do gray and red squirrels. Warblers and many other songbirds migrate through in May while the migration months of September and October are prime hawk-viewing times along the escarpment. Listen at night for great horned and barred owls, and watch for bats feeding on insects around electric lights. Geese and ducks use the lakes, and occasionally a common loon will stop during migration to rest and feed. Watch for sunfish nesting in the shallows; they are best seen with the aid of polarizing sunglasses.

Directions: *Traveling north on the New York State Thruway (Interstate 87) in southeastern New York, take Exit 20 at Saugerties. Turn onto Route 32 North for approximately 6 miles to Route 23A West. Go on Route 23A to the village of Haines Falls. Make the first right turn onto County Route 18, go 2 miles to the end of road. Traveling south on the Thruway, take Exit 21 at Catskill. Turn left onto Route 23 East and go to Route 9W South. Follow Route 9W through Catskill to Route 23A and follow the directions above.*

Ownership: NYS Department of Environmental Conservation 518-589-5058

Size: 600 acres   **Closest Town:** Haines Falls

Black bear are very much at home in New York's remote areas. About 3,600 live in the Adirondacks, 400 in the Catskills, and 100 in Allegany State Park. Sightings commonly occur in the Taconic Mountains and throughout the Southern Tier as well.

2. MINNEWASKA STATE PARK PRESERVE

Description: Located in the heart of the Northern Shawangunk Mountains, Minnewaska is a large "wilderness" park with many miles of trails and former carriage roads. The views from Lake Minnewaska, surrounded by white conglomerate cliffs, are extraordinary, as are the views from Hudson and Rondout Valley overlooks. The preserve offers hiking, picnicking, biking, cross-country skiing, and swimming, but no camping.

Viewing Information: Turkey vultures and ravens are two birds visitors can expect to see from the many scenic overlooks. In spring and fall, watch sharp-shinned, red-tailed, Cooper's, and broad-winged hawks. Winter wrens, Northern juncos, and several woodpeckers are among the many birds that nest here. Larger animals include white-tailed deer, coyotes, and an occasional bear. Cottontail rabbits inhabit the forest and Minnewaska is one of the more southerly habitats for the snowshoe hare. Also watch for ruffed grouse and wild turkey.

Directions: *From the New York State Thruway north of New York City, take New Paltz Exit 18. Turn west onto Route 299 West and go through New Paltz to a "T" intersection. Turn right onto Routes 44/55 and go 5 miles to park entrance (on left).*

Ownership: NYS Parks, Recreation and Historic Preservation; Administered by the Palisades Interstate Park Commission 914-255-0752

Size: 11,630 acres   **Closest Town:** New Paltz

With its short, rounded wings and long, rudderlike tail, the Cooper's hawk is built for the chase through the thickest woods. It follows every twist and turn to outfly fleeing birds, up to the size of robins and doves. Farmers have dubbed this bird the "chicken hawk," but most of them have never touched a chicken. The smaller but similar sharp-shinned hawk is the one sometimes seen feeding on visitors to backyard bird feeders. ARTHUR MORRIS

3. BASHAKILL WILDLIFE MANAGEMENT AREA

Description: One of the largest freshwater marshes in the state, the Bashakill is a premier viewing area for wetland wildlife. Surrounded by upland woods, the site provides ample opportunities for terrestrial wildlife viewing as well.

Viewing Information: The Bashakill WMA provides several ways to view wildlife: from the car, by boat (electric motors only), by canoe, on foot along an old railroad right-of-way with two observation towers, or along the D&H Canal towpath. White-tailed deer abound. Other mammals—you may only see traces of them—are beaver, muskrat, and otter. Watch for green and great blue herons hunting in the shallows and for osprey and bald eagle soaring overhead. Common moorhen nest among the water plants. Expect to see belted kingfisher rattle by overhead. Many migratory duck species use the marsh to nest or rest. May is the busiest viewing month.

Directions: *On Route 17 in Sullivan County in southeastern New York, exit at Wurtsboro. Take Route 209 South for 1.5 miles.*

Ownership: NYS Department of Environmental Conservation 914-256-3098

Size: 2,175 acres   **Closest Towns:** Westbrookville and Wurtsboro

By providing landscapes of alternating forest and clearings, we have encouraged the white-tailed deer. It occurs nearly everywhere in the state except on Manhattan Island. JIM ROETZEL

4. MONGAUP VALLEY WILDLIFE MANAGEMENT AREA, EAGLE OBSERVATION AREA

Description: When rivers and lakes freeze in the northern states and in Canada, bald eagles fly south to winter where open water for fishing can be found. Favorite wintering sites include the St. Lawrence River, the lower Hudson River, the upper Delaware River, and several Sullivan County reservoirs. Mongaup Falls Reservoir within the Mongaup Valley Wildlife Management Area (WMA) is especially attractive because water releases by the Orange and Rockland Utilities keep the river and reservoir from freezing completely, thus supplying abundant fish. A 10-foot by 20-foot building, enclosed on three sides, has been built at an optimum viewing site on Route 43. Contact the nearby Eldred Preserve for information on bald eagle conservation and educational programs, 914-557-8025.

Viewing Information: Eagles winter here from November through March, with the best viewing December through February. VISITORS MUST GO IMMEDIATELY INTO THE EAGLE OBSERVATION BUILDING FROM THE PARKING LOT. IF DISTURBED, EAGLES MAY LEAVE THE AREA.

Directions: *From the New York State Thruway (Interstate 87) take the Harriman Exit 16. Go west on Route 17 to Exit 105 and take Route 42 South through Monticello. Approximately 10 miles from Monticello, take a right turn onto County Route 43 and go 2 miles. The building is on the left.*

Ownership: NYS Department of Environmental Conservation (914) 256-3098

Size: 6,500 acres   **Closest Towns:** Forestburgh and Glen Spey

Though the bald eagle was eliminated by the 1960s as a breeding bird in New York by DDT, a reintroduction program has restored our national emblem to healthy numbers. Besides overwintering birds, people can observe nesting eagles at both Oak Orchard Wildlife Management Area and Montezuma National Wildlife Refuge.
JEFF LEPORE

REGION TWO: APPALACHIAN PLATEAU

Covering nearly 17,000 square miles, this is the state's largest ecozone. This zone also covers much of Pennsylvania. With a typical plateau structure of horizontal rock formations, the topography is irregular, with broadly rolling hills and steep valleys—much of it more than 1,000 feet above sea level. The Susquehanna and Delaware watersheds drain much of this zone. This is a landscape of active agriculture and abandoned farms as well as extensive forests. Black bear have begun to re-occupy many areas of this zone, but chances of seeing one are very slight. This is a land of "upland wildlife"—wild turkeys

and deer are abundant here; in early spring, you will often see them on south-facing slopes in large mixed groups of the two species. Grouse, woodcock, forest and forest-edge songbirds, and hawks are readily seen from public lands. Scenic vistas abound and many lightly traveled roads offer good opportunities to enjoy the view.

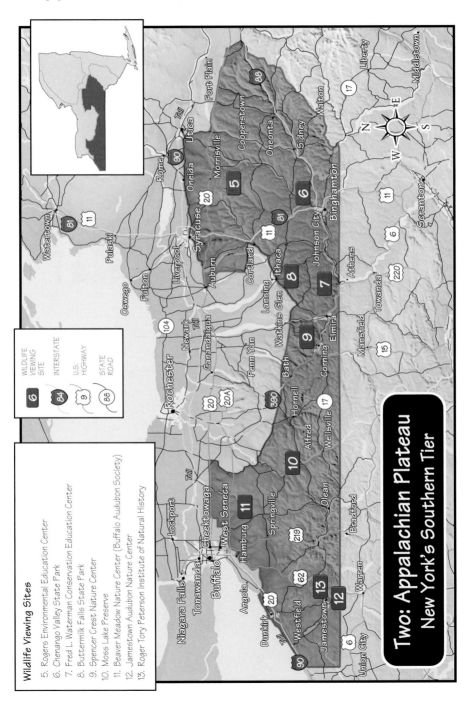

Wildlife Viewing Sites

5. Rogers Environmental Education Center
6. Chenango Valley State Park
7. Fred L. Waterman Conservation Education Center
8. Buttermilk Falls State Park
9. Spencer Crest Nature Center
10. Moss Lake Preserve
11. Beaver Meadow Nature Center (Buffalo Audubon Society)
12. Jamestown Audubon Nature Center
13. Roger Tory Peterson Institute of Natural History

WILDLIFE VIEWING SITE 6
INTERSTATE 84
U.S. HIGHWAY 9
STATE ROAD 88

Two: Appalachian Plateau
New York's Southern Tier

Description: The Rogers Center contains a number of wildlife habitats: mixed hardwood forest, spruce and pine plantations, old fields, wetlands, ponds, and river edge. As a result, the site attracts a large variety of wildlife. Trails through each of these habitats and a boardwalk through the wetland provide easy access to wildlife viewing. A trail on the south side of the highway winds uphill to the Farm Tower providing a panoramic view of the Chenango Valley. Picnic tables and a shelter encourage an extended visit. A visitor center with interactive exhibits is open all year.

Viewing Information: Mallard ducks and Canada geese are the most obvious birds throughout the year. Frogs, turtles, great blue herons, belted kingfishers, mink, and muskrats also utilize the wetlands. An indoor viewing area overlooking one of the center's ponds provides comfortable waterfowl and songbird viewing. Trout ponds permit easy viewing of several trout species. Sunfish, bullhead, and carp are also visible in the ponds. Contact the Rogers Center at the phone number below for a seasonal schedule of indoor programs and outdoor guided walks.

Directions: Sherburne is located on Route 12 midway between Binghamton and Utica in the east-central part of the state. From Sherburne, take Route 80 West one mile to the center entrance on the right.

Ownership: NYS Department of Environmental Conservation 607-674-4017

Size: 571 acres   **Closest Town:** Sherburne

The bluebird makes its home in open country. Numbers of our official state bird declined earlier in this century due to the replacement of nest hole–affording wood fence posts with metal ones, and to competition for nest sites with English sparrows and tree swallows. Thanks to the efforts of hundreds of volunteers who helped to place suitable nest boxes, bluebird numbers have significantly increased.
TOM VEZO

6. CHENANGO VALLEY STATE PARK

Description: Chenango Valley State Park is large and well developed with an 18-hole golf course, cabins, trailer and tent site camping, and a bathing area. Exhibits interpreting the park's natural history and brochures interpreting the three self-guided trails are found here.

Viewing Information: A number of bat shelters located next to the park's major buildings provide a unique chance to view wildlife. While slowly driving through the park, visitors often see deer, woodchuck, and wild turkey. At the lakes, you might see a great blue or green heron as well as Canada geese, mallards, wood ducks, and mergansers.

Directions: *From Interstate 88 north of Binghamton in south-central New York, take the Port Crane Exit 3. Turn left onto Route 369 North for about 4 miles to the park entrance.*

Ownership: NYS Parks, Recreation and Historic Preservation 607-648-5251

Size: 1,071 acres   **Closest Town:** Binghamton

7. FRED L. WATERMAN CONSERVATION EDUCATION CENTER

Description: Nestled in a wooded hilltop overlooking the Susquehanna River, this nonprofit community nature center offers 94 acres of mature woodland, fields, gardens, a gorge with a waterfall, and a bluebird trail—all connected by 5 miles of nature trails. The center's interpretive building contains a natural history museum, an auditorium, classrooms, a reference library, and a nature gift shop. Year-round programming and special events take place here.

Viewing Information: At the Waterman Center, follow the bluebird trail for good views of our state bird. In the Lolita Waterman Wildlife Garden watch for butterflies and ruby-throated hummingbirds visiting the flowers. The blind at Apalachin Marsh will help you get a good view of water and shore birds. Brick Pond is one of the best birding spots in the state. A boardwalk provides easy access. Inquire at the center's interpretive building about wildlife-watching boat tours of the river.

Directions: *From Route 17 west of Binghamton in south-central New York, take the Apalachin Exit 66. Turn right onto Route 434 and go 1.5 miles to Hilton Road. Go 0.5 miles to top of hill and turn left into parking lot.*

Ownership: Waterman Conservation Education Center, Inc. 607-625-2221

Size: 96 acres plus 210 acres in three outlying sites.

Closest Towns: Apalachin and Oswego

8. BUTTERMILK FALLS STATE PARK

Description: Located in the heart of the Finger Lakes, Buttermilk Falls is one of many gorges with waterfalls that cut through the native shales to the lake valley. Essentially a linear park, running more than 2 miles in length, it stretches from where Buttermilk Creek enters Treman Lake and then tumbles through a deep, wooded gorge past beautiful potholes and many waterfalls to spectacular Buttermilk Falls itself. Swimming is permitted in the falls plunge pool; cabins and tent sites are available.

Viewing Information: Muskrat, beaver, and mink are among the water mammals that utilize this waterway. Campers might expect to see skunk, raccoon, opossum, and red fox. Watch at dusk for little brown bats and big brown bats and flying squirrels. Coyotes can be heard some nights. Most obvious by day will be gray and red squirrels, chipmunks, and cottontail rabbits. Upland birds inhabiting the park are ruffed grouse and wild turkey. Songbirds abound during the migratory peak in mid-May. Watch overhead for sharp-shinned, red-tailed, and broad-winged hawks. Other noteworthy birds include pileated woodpecker, owls, and great blue heron. Ferns, mosses, and wildflowers add to the beauty of the cool, moist, shaded gorge. A trail brochure is available for the nature trail that encircles Larch Meadows wetland behind the ball fields not far from the park entrance.

Directions: *The park is in central New York, just south of Ithaca on Route 13.*

Ownership: NYS Parks, Recreation and Historic Preservation 607-387-7041

Size: 751 acres   **Closest Town:** Ithaca

The beaver, our official state mammal, remains active as long as its pond isn't frozen. During the winter, it carries food sticks from an adjacent food cache into its lodge. Beaver are among the few animals besides humans that alter their environment for their own benefit. Their dam-flooded ponds benefit dozens of other water-dependent animal species, as well. GERARD LEMMO

9. SPENCER CREST NATURE CENTER

Description: Located adjacent to Corning Community College atop Spencer Hill overlooking the town of Corning and the Chemung Valley, Spencer Crest is a unique habitat—the only site in New York where two forest zones intersect: an oak-hickory-hemlock forest and a beech-birch-maple forest. Wildlife watchers can explore the area on seven miles of foot trails. Adding to the diversity of the landscape are Amelia Pond, with its resident beaver, smaller Turtle Pond, the stream connecting them, and three large meadows.

Viewing Information: Be sure to check the feeding areas, where 11,000 pounds of sunflower seed and 4,500 pounds of shell corn attract large numbers of birds and mammals. The ponds are also wildlife meccas. Snapping turtles plumb the depths while painted turtles are fond of sunning on logs. Evidence of beavers is obvious; watch for swimming muskrat.

Directions: From Denison Parkway (Route 17) in Corning in south-central New York, turn up the hill on Walnut Street at the Post Office. At the top of Walnut Street veer right onto Powder House Road and continue up the hill about 1.5 miles to the stop sign. Go straight 0.25 mile to the nature center entrance on left.

Ownership: Spencer Crest Nature Center, Inc. 607-962-2169

Size: 250 acres   **Closest Town:** Corning

10. MOSS LAKE PRESERVE

Description: Designated a National Natural Landmark, this preserve's most outstanding feature is a 15-acre bog lake. A U-shaped boardwalk enables visitors to enjoy the bog's unusual flora, which includes insect-eating plants.

Viewing Information: At least 75 species of birds have been seen at the preserve. Canada geese, mallards, and wood ducks breed here; canvasbacks and redheads are noteworthy migrants.

Directions: From the New York State Thruway (Interstate 90) in western New York, take Exit 54 and then go southeast about 15 miles on Route 400 to Route 20A and then go east on US20A about 29 miles to Warsaw, and then south about 25 miles on Route 19 to Houghton. From the intersection of Route 19 and Genesee Street in Houghton, drive 1.4 miles south on Route 19. Turn right on Sand Hill Road, a dirt road, and drive 0.9 miles up the hill to the preserve on the left. From Route 17 (The Quickway), exit at Belvedere and drive 13 miles north on Route 19 to Houghton and follow directions above.

Ownership: The Nature Conservancy 716-546-8030

Size: 82 acres   **Closest Town:** Houghton

11. BEAVER MEADOW NATURE CENTER (BUFFALO AUDUBON SOCIETY)

Description: Visitors can explore the fields, forests, and ponds of this area on 7 miles of trails. An active beaver colony maintains the largest of Beaver Meadow's nine ponds. A special boardwalk trail provides access for persons with disabilities. At the Interpretive Visitor Center, open daily except Sundays, visitors may rent binoculars or snowshoes and borrow pond scoops.

Viewing Information: Hikers might see beaver and muskrat early in the morning or at dusk. Water birds are plentiful and easily seen. Deer are often encountered late in the day.

Directions: *The center is located in western New York's Wyoming County, southeast of Buffalo. From Buffalo take Route 400 to East Aurora Exit and then take Route 20A East 10 miles to the blinker light at Route 77. Turn onto Route 77 South. Go 7.5 miles to a left on Welch Road for 0.25 miles to the flagpole parking lot. From the south, take Route 98 North to blinking light at junction of Routes 77 and 78. Go through the light on Route 77 and go 1.5 miles to a right turn onto Welch Road to the flagpole parking lot.*

Ownership: Buffalo Audubon Society, Inc. 716-457-3228

Size: 324 acres   **Closest Town:** Java Center

12. JAMESTOWN AUDUBON NATURE CENTER

Description: The nature center includes the 600-acre Burgeson Wildlife Sanctuary and has 5 miles of trails through hardwood and coniferous forests and over boardwalks through marsh and swampland.

Viewing Information: A universal-access, hard-surfaced trail provides easy entry from the parking area to the nature interpretive building, herb and butterfly garden, amphitheater, and along Frog Pond Trail to an observation deck overlooking Big Pond. Fifteen river otters were released into Big Pond in 1996. Recreational activities include a canoe route on the Conewango River and a "Rails to Trails" multi-use trail—both 0.5 mile away.

Directions: *From points east: On Route 17 (Southern Tier Expressway) in Chautauqua County in southeastern New York, turn south onto Route 62 and go 10 miles through Frewsburg toward Warren, PA. South of Frewsburg, turn left onto Riverside Road and go 0.3 miles to the center entrance on the left. From Jamestown and points north and west: Take Route 60 South out of Jamestown to Route 62 South. Go south on Route 62 and follow the directions above.*

Ownership: Jamestown Audubon Society, Inc. 716-569-2345

Size: 600 acres   **Closest Town:** Jamestown

13. ROGER TORY PETERSON INSTITUTE OF NATURAL HISTORY

Description: The Roger Tory Peterson Institute is a national environmental education organization dedicated to instilling an appreciation and understanding of the natural world in children. It is named for the famous artist, naturalist, and author, and is located in the city of his birth.

Viewing Information: Since the institute's major wildlife emphasis is on interpretation through art, photography, and writing, visitors should visit the building—an architectural work of art in itself. Frequent exhibitions (a fee is charged) feature the work of Dr. Peterson and other wildlife artists. An interpretive trail provides guidance on plant and animal identification using the Peterson Field Guides. Trails wind through a variety of habitats including forest, field, and marsh. A special viewing site is a butterfly garden designed by Virginia Peterson. This garden attracts a variety of butterflies and ruby-throated hummingbirds throughout the growing season.

Directions: *In Chautauqua County in western New York, take the New York State Thruway (Interstate 90) westbound to Exit 59 and then south on route 60 to Jamestown. From the Southern Tier Expressway (Route 17), take Exit 12 then go south on Route 60 one mile to Jamestown. In Jamestown, take a left (east) on Buffalo Street, another left onto Falconer Street, and then take another left onto Curtis Street. The Institute entrance is on the left.*

Ownership: Roger Tory Peterson Institute of Natural History 716-665-2473

Size: 27 acres   **Closest Town:** Jamestown

Roger Tory Peterson relates this adventure with a northern flicker: He saw an inert lump of brown feathers, and figuring it was probably dead, "poked it. It was very much alive. The red stripe on the back of the neck showed, and its wild eyes, and he flashed away with his yellow wings. It was the contrast between death and life. Ever since, birds have been for me the most vivid symbol of life; they seem the most vital things." ROGER TORY PETERSON ILLUS.

33

REGION THREE: GREAT LAKES PLAIN

This flat plain borders Lake Erie, the Niagara Frontier, Lake Ontario and the St. Lawrence Valley. Elevations range from 245 feet, on the surface of Lake Ontario, up to 1000 feet, with most of the land under 800 feet. Proximity to the Great Lakes greatly moderates the climate here, the long growing season and mild winters are exceeded only in the Coastal Lowlands. Thousands of ducks and geese take advantage of this moderate climate to overwinter here, primarily in the Finger Lakes. With the lowest percentage of any zone in the state, only 20 percent is forested. It has the most extensive block of quality farmland with vegetable, grain, and fruit farms predominating. A narrow strip of land running the length of the southern shore of Lake Ontario provides critical habitat for many species of songbirds. Because the northern migration of these birds is blocked by the lake, they "funnel" along the lakeshore to its eastern end where they can cross into Canada and move on to their summer

breeding grounds. During this migration, chances of seeing them are great. Similarly, birds of prey perform spring migration spectaculars along the lake's shoreline. Marshy embayments (many with hillside overlooks) at several stretches along the lake front are superb places to find birds throughout much of the year, while a journey along the rocky, islanded St. Lawrence is not unlike a trip to the coast of Maine.

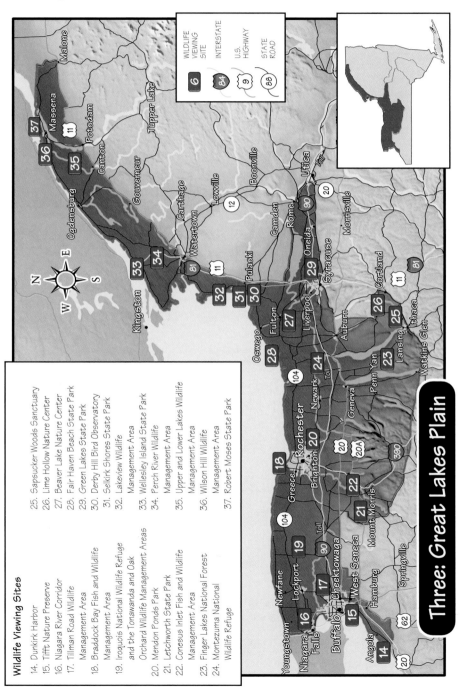

Wildlife Viewing Sites

14. Dunkirk Harbor
15. Tifft Nature Preserve
16. Niagara River Corridor
17. Tillman Road Wildlife Management Area
18. Braddock Bay Fish and Wildlife Management Area
19. Iroquois National Wildlife Refuge and the Tonawanda and Oak Orchard Wildlife Management Areas
20. Mendon Ponds Park
21. Letchworth State Park
22. Conesus Inlet Fish and Wildlife Management Area
23. Finger Lakes National Forest
24. Montezuma National Wildlife Refuge
25. Sapsucker Woods Sanctuary
26. Lime Hollow Nature Center
27. Beaver Lake Nature Center
28. Fair Haven Beach State Park
29. Green Lakes State Park
30. Derby Hill Bird Observatory
31. Selkirk Shores State Park
32. Lakeview Wildlife Management Area
33. Wellesley Island State Park
34. Perch River Wildlife Management Area
35. Upper and Lower Lakes Wildlife Management Area
36. Wilson Hill Wildlife Management Area
37. Robert Moses State Park

Three: Great Lakes Plain

35

14. DUNKIRK HARBOR

Description: The large Niagara Mohawk power plant at Dunkirk discharges warm water into the harbor, keeping it from freezing here in winter. Large numbers of gulls and ducks take advantage of this open water for winter feeding and resting, making bird watching excellent here during the fall, winter, and spring. A pier and walkway along the harbor provide excellent viewing opportunities.

Viewing Information: Open waters attract thousands of mergansers and hundreds of Bonaparte's gulls to the harbor each winter. Mallards, black ducks, Canada geese, and coots are almost always present in good numbers, too. Spring and fall visitors should travel 0.5 mile to the west along Point Drive North to Point Gratiot, a city park across the street from the U.S. Coast Guard Station's picturesque lighthouse. In this wooded park migrating songbirds gather to await the right weather conditions to fly across Lake Erie. Peak activity dates are May 12 to 15.

Directions: *From the New York State Thruway in Chautauqua County in western New York, take Exit 59 and drive west 2 miles to Central Avenue. Turn right onto Central Avenue and drive north to the lake front. The pier is at the north end of Central Avenue.*

Ownership: The City of Dunkirk 716-366-6200 and Niagara Mohawk Corp.

Size: N/A   **Closest Town:** Dunkirk

15. TIFFT NATURE PRESERVE

Description: Only 3 miles from downtown Buffalo, this wilderness oasis contrasts sharply with the factories, grain elevators, and railyards of Buffalo's adjacent waterfront.

Viewing Information: Tifft Nature Preserve is a beautifully restored natural area with forest, fields, ponds, and cattail marsh. Take the boardwalk out onto the 75-acre cattail marsh, the preserve's most prominent feature. Note the muskrat lodges here. You might see a muskrat swimming, head and tail visible. The Makowski Visitor Center welcomes visitors Tuesdays through Sundays. Fishing is another popular activity.

Directions: *From downtown Buffalo, travel south on Route 5 West to Fuhrmann Boulevard South. Turn left onto Tifft Street. Turn left onto Fuhrmann Boulevard North (also called Ohio Street). The preserve is 0.4 miles north of this intersection.*

Ownership: City of Buffalo. Administered by Buffalo Museum of Science, 716-896-5200 weekdays, 716-825-6397 weekends

Size: 264 acres   **Closest Town:** Buffalo

16. NIAGARA RIVER CORRIDOR

Description: The Niagara Frontier State Park Region includes 14 sites, beginning on Lake Erie and continuing north along the Niagara River to Lake Ontario. The Robert Moses State Parkway provides a unique opportunity for wildlife watchers to quickly and conveniently visit many of these parks and habitats and to see a wide variety of aquatic and upland animals, even in a single day. The following are especially recommended for wildlife viewing. Beaver Island and Buckhorn Island state parks on Grand Island in the Niagara River, which are connected by the West River Parkway which has two pull-off sites for water bird viewing. Earl W. Brydges Artpark, and Joseph Davis and Fort Niagara state parks, located north along the Niagara Gorge, each have their own distinctive attractions and mix of wildlife. To the east along Lake Ontario, visitors can explore Fort Niagara's Four Mile Creek State Park Campground and Wilson-Tuscarora State Park. Nature centers are located at Beaver Island and at Fort Niagara.

Viewing Information: Connecting 2 of the Great Lakes—Erie and Ontario, the Niagara River Corridor is both home to and migration route for large numbers of wildlife. A variety of bird species are found here, especially water birds.

Directions: *The Niagara Frontier State Park Region is located to the northwest of Buffalo. From the New York Thruway south of Buffalo, take Interstate 190. Signs along I-190 will direct you to Beaver Island and Buckhorn State Parks and the Niagara Reservation. Continue on I-190 North to Robert Moses Parkway exit. Take Robert Moses Parkway North to Fort Niagara on Lake Ontario. Access to most of the corridor's state parks is from the Robert Moses Parkway. If you are approaching Buffalo from the east on I-90, take I-290 to I-190 and follow the instructions above.*

Ownership: NYS Parks, Recreation and Historic Preservation 716-278-1780

Size: N/A   **Closest Town:** Niagara Falls

Best known as a mecca for honeymooners, Niagara Falls is part of an officially designated Important Bird Area, having many ducks and nineteen species of gulls.

FRANK KNIGHT

17. TILLMAN ROAD WILDLIFE MANAGEMENT AREA

Description: Only 8 miles east of the City of Buffalo, Tillman Road Wildlife Management Area is a wet lowland. Parking areas are located on Bergtold Road and on Tillman Road. Two hiking trails and a self-guided nature loop trail provide access, and a boardwalk with a viewing platform is located at the Bergtold Road entrance.

Viewing Information: This area's most prominent feature is an 80-acre cattail marsh which attracts large numbers of waterfowl during the spring and fall migrations. Amphibian watching is excellent for salamanders and seven frogs—spring peeper, green, bull, wood, chorus, northern leopard, and gray tree.

Directions: *In Erie County in western New York, take the New York State Thruway (Interstate 90) to Exit 49. Take Route 78 South (Transit Road) to Route 33, then east on Route 33 to Ransom Road. Continue north on Ransom Road to Tillman Road or to Bergtold Road. Turn left from either road into a parking area.*

Ownership: NYS Department of Environmental Conservation 716-851-7010

Size: 235 acres   **Closest Town:** Clarence

18. BRADDOCK BAY FISH AND WILDLIFE MANAGEMENT AREA

Description: This shallow-water, bay-marsh complex unique to Lake Ontario's south shoreline, located just west of Rochester, provides excellent waterfowl habitat. Roadways provide easy access.

Viewing Information: During the spring and fall migrations, all waterfowl common to the Atlantic Flyway may be observed. For an exciting double feature, visit Braddock Bay in late April to see thousands of ducks while migrating hawks and eagles numbering hundreds or thousands soar overhead. Watch waterfowl at stops along Lake Ontario State Parkway Westbound where it crosses Long Pond and at Button Wood and Salmon Creek. Edgemere Drive along the barrier bar provides great views of Buck Pond. Watch the hawks from the observation tower and the west spit at Braddock Bay Park.

Directions: *From Rochester in Monroe County, take Route 104 West to Route 390 North. Turn west on the Lake Ontario State Parkway. Turn right onto Long Pond Road for access to Edgemere Road on the barrier bar, or continue on the parkway past Long Pond to Manitou Beach Road and turn right into Braddock Bay Park.*

Ownership: NYS Department of Environmental Conservation 716-226-2466 and the Town of Greece 716-225-2000

Size: 2,500 acres   **Closest Towns:** Rochester and Greece

19. IROQUOIS NATIONAL WILDLIFE REFUGE AND THE TONAWANDA & OAK ORCHARD WILDLIFE MANAGEMENT AREAS

Description: Oak Orchard Swamp is a historic wetland area in west-central New York used by waterfowl and native peoples long before European settlement.

Viewing Information: Habitat enhancement brings tens of thousands of waterfowl here for exciting wildlife viewing from numerous parking areas and overlooks. More than 29 ducks, geese, and swans are among the more than 250 species of birds identified here. The first two weeks in April offer peak viewing of more than 40,000 geese and 4,000 ducks. Expect to see fewer geese (about 7,500), and more ducks (about 8,000) mid-September through November. Thrushes, warblers, and shore birds are also abundant. Red-tailed hawks and kestrels patrol overhead. Occasional northern harriers, ospreys, and bald eagles are seen. April through July, watch an active bald eagle nest on a closed-circuit TV monitor at the Iroquois refuge headquarters. Upland birds include ring-necked pheasants, ruffed grouse, and woodcocks. Common mammals include muskrat, beaver, mink, raccoon, white-tailed deer, opossum, red and gray fox, squirrels, rabbits, and woodchucks.

Directions: *In western New York, take Exit 48A on the New York State Thruway (Interstate 90) to Route 77. Proceed 12 miles north on Route 77 to information sign at Casey Road.*

Ownership: U.S. Fish and Wildlife Service (Iroquois) 716-948-5445, NYS Department of Environmental Conservation (Tonawanda & Oak Orchard) 716-948-5182

Size: Iroquois: 10,818 acres, Tonawanda WMA: 5,600 acres, Oak Orchard: 2,500 acres   **Closest Town:** Alabama

GREAT LAKES PLAIN

Oak Orchard Marsh offers excellent waterfowl watching spring and fall. FRANK KNIGHT

20. MENDON PONDS PARK

Description: Mendon Ponds offers year-round recreational programming, and is well known for its wealth of geologic and wildlife resources. The park is listed on the National Registry of Natural Landmarks for its many glacial features including kames, kettles, and eskers. Exhibits at the Mendon Ponds Nature Center explain the glacial geology and describe the diverse mix of plants and animals that inhabit the park. The nature center offers school, youth, and adult programs throughout the year. The many miles of trails are popular with hikers and cross-country skiers.

Viewing Information: The park enjoys a reputation for great birding all year. In the winter, carry sunflower seed with you along the Bird Song Trail behind the nature center; the birds have become accustomed to being hand fed. Expect to be pursued down the trail by chickadees, red-breasted nuthatches, and tufted titmice until you feed them. A walk around the loop trail between Hopkins Point and Deep Pond in May can treat experienced birders to sightings of more than 100 upland and water bird species. Wood ducks and mallards nest in the many wet areas where evidence of beavers abounds. Upland wildlife includes deer, turkeys, red fox, red and gray squirrels, and chipmunks. Butterfly weed and other wildflowers in the open areas attract a variety of butterflies.

Directions: *From the New York State Thruway (Interstate 90) in western New York, Exit 45 or 46, go 8 miles on Route 65 South (Clover Street) to park entrance.*

Ownership: Monroe County Parks Department 716-256-4954; Mendon Ponds Nature Center 716-334-3780

Size: 2,550 acres   **Closest Town:** Honeoye Falls and Pittsford

Look for caterpillars of the monarch butterfly feeding on milkweed during the summer months. In the fall enjoy the southward migration flights of adults all across the state. TOM VEZO

40

21. LETCHWORTH STATE PARK

Description: Called the "Grand Canyon of the East," Letchworth is a large and beautiful park featuring the north-flowing Genesee River at the bottom of a 400- to 500-foot cliff. Overlooks provide spectacular views of three waterfalls. Foot paths and auto roads parallel the river and pass the historic Glen Iris Inn and Seneca Indian sites. The William Pryor Letchworth Museum provides an excellent introduction to the park. Picnic areas, swimming pools, a campground, and 82 cabins entice visitors to extend their visit. Stop at the park visitor center for a copy of *The Genesee Naturalist,* a quarterly nature booklet containing natural history information listing interpretive programs.

Viewing Information: At any of the gorge overlooks, expect to see turkey vultures perched on cliffside trees or soaring overhead. Plan a visit for a moonlit spring evening to hear red fox and coyote. Watch for wild turkey crossing roads and trails. White-tailed deer, cottontail rabbits, and woodchucks can also be seen on roadsides. Common mergansers and wood ducks are the most abundant among the several ducks visible on the river. Watch for beavers along the river, as well. Bald eagles use the river year-round, but the red-tailed hawk is a more commonly seen raptor.

Directions: *From Interstate 390 south of Rochester, take Exit 7 (Mt. Morris) to Route 36 North. Follow signs on Route 36 to park entrance.*

Ownership: NYS Parks, Recreation and Historic Preservation 716-493-3600

Size: 14,340 acres   **Closest Towns:** Castile, Mt. Morris, Perry, Portageville

Watch for wild turkeys feeding at wood edges and farm fields across the state. Beechnuts and acorns on the forest floor and corn gleaned from harvested fields are its diet staples.

BILL BANASZEWSKI

22. CONESUS INLET FISH AND WILDLIFE MANAGEMENT AREA

Description: Located at the south end of Conesus Lake, the westernmost of the Finger Lakes, this picturesque wetland community contains many wetland impoundments. The largest covers 400 acres. Managed for public use and the enjoyment of wildlife, this is excellent habitat for water birds and wildlife viewing. Unique opportunities to view spawning runs of walleye and northern pike make this a popular area attraction.

Viewing Information: A flat valley floodplain with rich marshes, ponds, and upland fields is cradled between steep-sloping forested hills. Abundant and diverse wildlife abound. Migrating waterfowl dominate spring and fall. Wildlife viewers in spring and summer are welcomed by the sounds of secretive marsh birds like common moorhens, rails, and grebes. A great blue heron rookery provides additional viewing. Raptors are common. Red-tailed hawks nest here and harriers, screech-owls, and others are often seen. More than 30 nest boxes attract Eastern bluebirds, and an overwintering population enables year-round viewing of our state bird. Mammals such as beavers, cottontail rabbits, muskrats, fox, and deer leave tracks and traces for visitors to find. Reptiles and amphibians are seasonally abundant. A chorus of spring peepers, tree frogs, and bullfrogs can be almost deafening in the spring, and leopard frogs leap away with every step in late July. This site's most unusual wildlife viewing occurs during spring spawning season when walleye cluster along the shallows of clear-flowing South McMillan Creek. Pike also use the diked spawning beds designed expressly for them. Six shallow-water impoundments total 500 acres with more than a mile of dike to walk and explore. A mile-long trail follows the west side of the largest wetland where walkers can enjoy the riparian woods and wetland scenery.

Directions: *From Interstate 390, south of Rochester and Interstate 90, take Route 15 South (Exit 9). Continue on Route 15 to Route 256 South to the wildlife management area.*

Ownership: NYS Department of Environmental Conservation 716-226-2466

Size: 1,120 acres   **Closest Town:** Conesus

The bullfrog's vibrant bass notes, sounding like "jug-o-rum," help viewers locate our largest frog. Look for them at lakes, ponds, bogs, and sluggish portions of streams.
THOMAS D. LINDSAY

42

23. FINGER LAKES NATIONAL FOREST

Description: New York State's only National Forest, this multi-use land is unique to the National Forest system in the East, with roadways on 1-mile-square grids and views of pastured cattle. Recreation opportunities include auto access, camping, hiking, berry picking, cross-country skiing, horseback riding, and snowmobiling. Visitors should stop at the visitor center for a map with recommendations for areas to visit for wildlife viewing.

Viewing Information: With an extensive network of roads, much wildlife viewing can be done through your car window. Turkey and white-tailed deer are two animals easily observed from the car. A number of ponds dot the forest and wood-duck boxes have been placed to encourage nesting. Some of the ponds have lodges, dams, and an active beaver population. Kestrel boxes attract these small birds of prey. In the open areas, look and listen for ring-necked pheasant, eastern meadowlark, and American woodcock. The latter puts on a fascinating, easy to see and hear courtship display at dusk in the spring. Dusk is also a good time to see the striped skunk and red fox along roadways. Listen in the evening for the calls of the screech, barred, and great horned owls.

Directions: *Finger Lakes National Forest is located in south-central New York's Finger Lakes Region between Seneca and Cayuga Lakes. From the New York State Thruway (Interstate 90), take the Seneca Falls Exit 41 and go south on Route 414 to Hector. From Ithaca, take Route 79 North to Route 414 North to Hector and the visitor center.*

Ownership: United States Department of Agriculture Forest Service 607-546-4470

Size: 15,489 acres   **Closest Town:** Hector

The red-bellied woodpecker's name is somewhat misleading. The "red" on the belly is more a light tinge; the bright red is limited to the crown and nape of males and the nape of females. A resident of open woodlands, suburbs, and parks, the red-bellied's chortling call is reminiscent of a raccoon's. JIM ROETZEL

24. MONTEZUMA NATIONAL WILDLIFE REFUGE

Description: Located in the middle of one of the most active flight lanes in the Atlantic Flyway, Montezuma is the premier waterfowl watching site in upstate New York. The refuge's 3,500 acres of diked pools provide resting, feeding, and nesting habitat for migratory birds. Begun in 1976, a cooperative reintroduction program with the NYS Department of Environmental Conservation has resulted in bald eagles once again successfully rearing young at Montezuma. The visitor center has exhibits, leaflets, and an observation deck to enhance the visitor's experience. A 3.5-mile Wildlife Drive provides easy access to all the pools and two observation towers.

Viewing Information: Mid-August through mid-October are peak sandpiper viewing times on exposed mudflats. Early morning and late afternoon from mid-September to late November afford spectacular views of up to 50,000 Canada geese and 150,000 ducks. The self-guiding Wildlife Drive is generally closed to traffic during the winter. From late February through April, the refuge hosts 85,000 Canada geese and 12,000 snow geese. In mid-May, warbler and songbird migration peaks along the Esker Brook Trail, where wildflower viewing is also great. Watch over the ponds for feeding osprey.

Directions: *From the New York State Thruway (Interstate 90), take the Seneca Falls Exit 41. The refuge is 5 miles east of Seneca Falls on Routes 5/20.*

Ownership: U.S. Fish and Wildlife Service 315-568-5987

Size: More than 7,000 acres   **Closest Town:** Seneca Falls

The redhead duck is one of several prairie slough and pothole ducks that rest and feed in central New York on their annual spring migration to breeding sites further west. They dive for submerged vegetation, insects, crustaceans, and snails. TOM VEZO

25. SAPSUCKER WOODS SANCTUARY

Description: The Cornell Laboratory of Ornithology at Sapsucker Woods is a world center for the study, appreciation, and conservation of birds. The site has 4.2 miles of trails through an upland hardwood forest, with a boardwalk through the woodland swamp for easy wildlife viewing. The Stuart Observatory overlooks a waterfowl pond and bird-feeding garden.

Viewing Information: More than 225 species of birds have been recorded at the sanctuary, and a checklist is available for you to record your finds. May is the best time to visit—the woodland is alive with migrating songbirds and spring wildflowers. Ducks, geese, and wading birds may be watched from the comfort of the indoor observatory where outdoor sounds are piped in.

Directions: *From Ithaca in central New York, take Route 13 North. Turn right onto Warren Road, then turn left (at the four-way stop) onto Hanshaw Road. Continue 0.8 miles on Hanshaw Road, then turn left onto Sapsucker Woods Road. The sanctuary is 0.8 miles on the left.*

Ownership: Cornell Laboratory of Ornithology 607-254-2473

Size: 220 acres   **Closest Town:** Ithaca

26. LIME HOLLOW NATURE CENTER

Description: Only 2 miles from the city of Cortland, Lime Hollow Nature Center (LHNC) is named for an open valley from whose marl ponds early settlers extracted agricultural lime.

Viewing Information: Five loop trails, from the 0.3-mile Sunset Trail to the 1-mile Brookside and 1.5-mile Mill Pond Trails, fit every interest and ability. At Cattail Pond near the visitor center enjoy wildlife viewing from the beautifully interpreted blind. A good sampling on a spring walk might include Canada geese, mallards, black and wood ducks, and hooded mergansers. Listen at dusk for great horned, screech and barred owls, and watch for flying squirrels. Turkey, ruffed grouse, deer, skunk, and red fox are year-round residents.

Directions: *From Cortland in central New York, Lime Hollow is just over 2 miles southwest. From Cortland, follow Route 13 South toward Dryden. Pass Lime Hollow Road on the right and take the next right, Gracie Road, to the Nature Center parking area on the left.*

Ownership: Lime Hollow Nature Center, Inc. and U.S. Fish and Wildlife Service 607-758-5462

Size: 115 acres   **Closest Town:** Cortland

27. BEAVER LAKE NATURE CENTER

Description: Northern hardwood, oak-hickory, and mixed forests, along with pine plantations, meadows, wetlands, and the 200-acre glacial lake, all connected by 8 miles of walking trails, make Beaver Lake Nature Center one of central New York's outstanding wildlife viewing facilities. Interpretive signs, telescopes, an observation tower, and a wildlife blind enhance the viewing experience for visitors.

Viewing Information: Beaver Lake provides a focus for wildlife viewing. Thousands of Canada geese use the lake spring and fall. Watch for great blue herons, belted kingfishers, double-crested cormorants, and an occasional osprey. In summer, rental canoes are available for exploring the lake. Look for beaver, muskrat, and mink. Be sure to explore the bog from a floating boardwalk where you might see water snakes, painted and snapping turtles, and bull and green frogs. Expect to see chipmunks and both gray and red squirrels in the forest and be alert for white-tailed deer, woodchucks, raccoons, fox, and eastern coyotes.

Directions: *From Baldwinsville in central New York northwest of Syracuse, drive approximately 4 miles west on Route 370 to a right turn onto East Mud Lake Road to the center entrance. From Exit 39 on the New York State Thruway (Interstate 90), take Route 690 North to the Beaver Lake/Route 370 Exit, then 2 miles west on Route 370 and right onto East Mud Lake Road to the center entrance.*

Ownership: Onondaga County 315-638-2519

Size: 650 acres　　　**Closest Town:** Baldwinsville

A large rodent of open farm country, the woodchuck is despised by farmers since their holes are hazards to farm equipment and livestock legs. A favored food of the coyote, woodchuck populations have been kept in check in recent years. Active by day in the summer, they hibernate during the winter months. GERARD LEMMO

28. FAIR HAVEN BEACH STATE PARK

Description: On the southeastern shore of Lake Ontario, Fair Haven Beach State Park contains hilly woodlands, sandy beach, and lakeshore bluffs. The park also fronts on Little Sodus Bay. Immediately behind the beach is Sterling Pond and Sterling Marsh. Tent and RV campsites and cabins are available. The short, self-guided Nature Trail and the longer Lakeshore Trail provide access to wildlife viewing.

Viewing Information: Fair Haven is a true haven for about 25 species of geese and ducks. Among the most common are Canada geese, wood ducks, black and ring-necked ducks, and mallards. Northern harriers and osprey are among the ten birds of prey often seen here. Watch for deer and squirrels along the Nature and Lakeshore trails.

Directions: *The park entrance is in the village of Fair Haven northeast of Syracuse in central New York, 15 miles west of Oswego on Route 104A.*

Ownership: NYS Parks, Recreation and Historic Preservation 315-947-5205

Size: 865 acres   **Closest Town:** Fair Haven

29. GREEN LAKES STATE PARK

Description: A state park since 1928 when 500 acres were purchased, Green Lakes includes two unique nearly 200-foot-deep, blue-green glacial lakes. Round Lake is a registered National Natural Landmark and is surrounded by an old-growth forest of enormous hemlocks and tulip trees. Green Lake has a popular beach, an 18-hole golf course, 137 campsites, seven cabins, and a nature center. Picnic areas, pavilions, boat rental, a concession stand, and 17 miles of trails round out the park's facilities.

Viewing Information: Wildlife can best be observed from the park's hiking and cross-country ski trails. The most popular viewing sites are on trails around both lakes. Canada geese, ducks, herons, and kingfishers feed in the lakes. Mammals include deer, woodchucks, raccoons, red and gray fox, coyotes, mink, skunks, cottontail rabbits, chipmunks, and red and gray squirrels.

Directions: *From the New York State Thruway (Interstate 90) in central New York, take Exit 34A to Interstate 481 South to Kirkville Road. Turn left and go east on Kirkville Road and then turn right onto Fremont Road. Then turn left onto Route 290 and go 3.5 miles to the park entrance.*

Ownership: NYS Parks, Recreation and Historic Preservation 315-637-6111

Size: 1,700 acres   **Closest Town:** Fayetteville

30. DERBY HILL BIRD OBSERVATORY

Description: Located in the southeast corner of Lake Ontario, Derby Hill is ideally located for observing the spring migration of hawks. When northbound hawks reach the lakeshore they turn east and north to take advantage of the rising air masses, called thermals, along the shore. The best hawk viewing is from a field adjacent to the lake shore. Two other viewing areas, South Lookout and Sage Creek Marsh are located along the access road, Sage Creek Drive.

Viewing Information: One of the premier birding sites in the northeast, Derby Hill enables visitors to see the 15 species of migrating hawks, vultures, and eagles that migrate through the state each year. Peak flights usually occur during the last ten days of April. The flights can be spectacular. More than 18,000 broad-winged hawks have been counted in a single day. A trail and boardwalk through field, wet meadow, and forest provide good songbird and other wildlife viewing.

Directions: From Interstate 81, take Mexico Exit north of Syracuse. Travel 5 miles west on Route 104 to Mexico. Then go 4 miles north on Route 3 to Route 104B West 0.75 miles to Sage Creek Drive. Follow the signs to the sanctuary.

Ownership: Onondaga Audubon Society 315-457-7731

Size: 50 acres   **Closest Town:** Mexico

31. SELKIRK SHORES STATE PARK

Description: Bordered on the north by the Salmon River and its marsh, on the south by Grindstone Creek and its marsh, and on the west by Lake Ontario's bluffs and beaches, Selkirk Shores State Park has a rich variety of wildlife habitats. Cabins and tent and trailer campsites are located near the lake. A network of hiking and cross-country ski trails winds through forests and fields.

Viewing Information: Ask at the park office for the checklist of more than 200 bird species recorded in the park. Spring migrations are spectacular as birds follow the shoreline to avoid the long lake crossing. Noteworthy are the early spring flights of hawks and eagles. Deer are common. Huge salmon migrate up the Salmon River to spawn each fall and steelhead trout in late fall and winter. Northern pike are common during the spring and summer.

Directions: From Pulaski in central New York north of Syracuse, take Exit 36 off of Interstate 81 and then Route 13 West to Route 3 South 1.5 miles to the park entrance.

Ownership: NYS Parks, Recreation and Historic Preservation 315-298-5737

Size: 980 acres   **Closest Town:** Port Ontario

32. LAKEVIEW WILDLIFE MANAGEMENT AREA

Description: Lakeview has diverse habitats including open field, shrubland, woodland, wetland, and natural-barrier beach. Public-use restrictions apply to the sensitive natural-barrier beach system. Lakeview's wetlands, protected from Lake Ontario storms by 4.5 miles of natural-barrier beach, are fed by Sandy and South Sandy creeks. The wetlands include emergent marshes and five separate ponds. Canoe and small boat launches enable access to water areas. An observation tower overlooks South Colwell Pond off Montario Point Road. Southwicks Beach State Park, north of the wildlife management area, offers picnicking, swimming, and camping. A self-guided nature trail through upland, wetland, and barrier-beach habitat can be accessed from the entrance road to the state park.

Viewing Information: Lakeview's wetlands attract many species of birds. Great blue and green herons and black-crowned night herons are present, as well as common moorhens and American bitterns. Mallards, blue-winged teal, and wood ducks are common. Birds of special interest are common, black, and Caspian terns. Reptiles and amphibians are well represented in the wetlands: painted and snapping turtles; northern water snakes; and green, tree, and leopard frogs. Common mammals include muskrats, beavers, white-tailed deer, red fox, coyotes, gray squirrels, and cottontail rabbits. Expect to see steelhead trout and chinook salmon run South Sandy and Sandy creeks in the fall.

Directions: From Interstate 81 in north-central New York, take the Pulaski Exit 36. Then take Route 13 West to Route 3. Turn right on Route 3 and go north approximately 10 miles to the wildlife management area.

Ownership: NYS Department of Environmental Conservation 315-785-2261

Size: 3,400 acres   **Closest Town:** Ellisburg

GREAT LAKES PLAIN

The green heron catches fish, water snakes, grasshoppers, crayfish, mice, frogs, and other small animals with a lightning-like thrust of its beak. JOHN HEIDECKER

33. WELLESLEY ISLAND STATE PARK

Description: Wellesley Island sits in the St. Lawrence River near Lake Ontario's outflow, an ideal location for large numbers of wildlife. Steep cliffs and exposed rocky knobs give way to more gentle landscapes with wetlands, meadows and forests. At the 600-acre Minna Anthony Common Nature Center, a museum offers displays on the St. Lawrence River environment. A full schedule of educational and recreational programs are offered.

Viewing Information: With more than 8 miles of trails winding through shoreline habitats, marshes, fields, and forests, wildlife viewing opportunities abound. Gulls will be most obvious along the shore. You might see great black-backed, herring and ring-billed gulls, common terns, and, less frequently, Caspian terns. Look for sanderlings, semi-palmated and spotted sandpipers at the water's edge. Watch in the marsh for green and bull frogs, painted and snapping turtles. Most impressive are the great blue and green herons. Around dawn and dusk, deer can be seen in the forest and clearings. Woodchucks can be seen throughout the day. Ruffed grouse and turkey are among the largest forest birds. Several species of hawks take advantage of the island's abundant rodent population. Osprey are common over the water.

Directions: In north central New York, take Interstate 81 for 24 miles north of Watertown. Cross the Thousand Island Bridge to the first exit and follow the signs to the state park.

Ownership: NYS Parks, Recreation and Historic Preservation 315-482-2479

Size: 2,643 acres   **Closest Town:** Alexandria Bay

Herring gulls feed on fish, crustaceans, marine worms, shellfish, sea urchins, and insects. Adults regurgitate liquefied food in response to young tapping on the red spot near the bill tip. TOM VEZO

34. PERCH RIVER WILDLIFE MANAGEMENT AREA

Description: Diverse habitats including open field, shrubland, woodland and wetland characterize Perch River Wildlife Management Area (WMA). The wetlands include open water, emergent marsh, thicket and wooded swamp. The WMA is divided into three zones according to use: public, wetland restricted, and refuge. Public-use zones are open all year, while access to the wetland restricted zones is by permit only. The refuge zone is closed to public use except for a controlled ice-fishing program on the Perch Lake refuge. An observation tower off of Vaadi Road overlooks Stone Mills Pool.

Viewing Information: Perch River's pools and wetlands attract large numbers and varieties of bird life. Bald eagles, ospreys, and black terns nest here. Canada geese and mute swans are the largest birds on the water. A few tundra swan are sometimes seen. Mallards, black and wood ducks, and blue-winged teal are common. Smaller waders include the spotted, upland, and solitary sandpipers. There is also a good chance of seeing greater and lesser yellowlegs. Scan the marsh and fields for some unusual small birds: marsh wren, Henslow's and grasshopper sparrows. Common water mammals include the muskrat, mink, and beaver. Early spring provides the best chance of seeing a river otter. Gray squirrels, white-tailed deer, red fox, coyotes, and cottontail rabbits are common throughout the area.

Directions: *From Interstate 81 in north-central New York near Watertown, take Exit 47. Take Route 12 North approximately 6 miles to signs and parking areas.*

Ownership: NYS Department of Environmental Conservation 315-785-2261

Size: 7,800 acres **Closest Town:** Watertown

Found in wooded and farm lands where grouse and rabbits are also abundant, the red fox is one of the world's best mousers. Active year-round (mostly at night), they also eat carrion and fruit.
GERARD LEMMO

GREAT LAKES PLAIN

35. UPPER AND LOWER LAKES WILDLIFE MANAGEMENT AREA

Description: Upper and Lower Lakes Wildlife Management Area (WMA) is a large waterfowl refuge lying between the Grasse River and Oswegatchie River. An observation tower overlooks Lower Lake and a boat ramp provides access to the Grasse River at the north end of the site.

Viewing Information: While most of the site is a wildlife refuge, access for seasonal hunting and recreational use by permit is maintained on three sides. The privately owned, publicly accessible Indian Creek Nature Center occupies the fourth side, with trails and boardwalks leading through prime viewing areas. The nature center has a viewing platform, bird blind, observation tower, picnic pavilion, and a small building with interpretive exhibits used by school children and other groups. A boardwalk and restroom are accessible to persons with disabilities. Spectacular flights of waterfowl may be seen in the fall. Pied-billed grebes dive for fish. Bitterns and great blue herons wade the marshes. Northern harriers patrol low over the open areas in search of meadow mice and rabbits.

Directions: From Canton northwest of the Adirondacks, take Route 68 two miles north. To reach the nature center, continue north on Route 68 to a left turn onto County Road 14 to the center entrance on the left.

Ownership: NYS Department of Environmental Conservation 315-386-4546; Indian Creek Nature Center 315-265-4879. Leased from NYS DEC and managed by the North Country Conservation Education Association

Size: 8,600 acres   **Closest Town:** Canton

With an abundance of water throughout the year, marshlands are among the most productive habitats in the world—both in vegetation and in wildlife diversity.

FRANK KNIGHT

36. WILSON HILL WILDLIFE MANAGEMENT AREA

Description: Wilson Hill contains three large, open pools and their surrounding wooded and open uplands: Bradford Point Pool, West Pool, and the Refuge Pool on the south shore of the St. Lawrence River. Wilson Hill is closed for most of the spring and summer. However, two observation towers are open year-round. One of the towers overlooks the Refuge Pool from Route 131. The other tower is located nearby off Willard Road and is accessible by way of a short nature trail. Several parking areas provide easy access to the entire area.

Viewing Information: At least a dozen species of duck can be seen on the ponds; viewing is best from the observation tower on Route 131. Flights of Canada and snow geese are spectacular in October. Watch for merlin over fields and water. Both wild turkey and ruffed grouse may be seen along the nature trail, especially in the morning. Listen for great horned and barred owls in the evening. Phone the Watertown Department of Environmental Conservation office for the July date of the goose drive and roundup. Otherwise, fall is the best time to visit.

Directions: *Massena is located north of the Adirondacks near the St. Lawrence River. Take Route 131 seven miles west of Massena to the management area.*

Ownership: NYS Department of Environmental Conservation 315-785-2261

Size: 3,526 acres　　**Closest Town:** Massena

37. ROBERT MOSES STATE PARK

Description: The second largest park in the Thousand Islands Region, Robert Moses has much to offer in addition to wildlife viewing: cabins, camping, recreation programs, picnic and beach areas, boat ramps, hiking trails, and an interpretive nature center. Roadways, trails, and parking are located both on the mainland and on Barnhart Island in the St. Lawrence River. Features include the power dam, the Eisenhower Lock, and the Long Sault Spillway Dam.

Viewing Information: Wildlife abounds at Robert Moses. White-tailed deer, woodchucks, raccoons, and red squirrels are common. Beaver inhabit the wetlands. The rich variety of waterfowl includes mallard, wood duck, hooded merganser, American wigeon, pintail, brant, and Canada and snow geese. Perch, pike, and largemouth bass can be seen in the river.

Directions: *Robert Moses State Park is located north of the Adirondacks near the St. Lawrence River. From Route 37 northeast of Massena, travel 2 miles to the 3-mile park access road.*

Ownership: NYS Parks, Recreation and Historic Preservation 315-769-8663

Size: 2,322 acres　　**Closest Town:** Massena

REGION FOUR: ADIRONDACKS

Characterized by long winters with heavy snowfall and a short, cool growing season, the Adirondack Park is largely protected in the "forever wild" New York Forest Preserve. Besides the black bears, pine martens, and fishers that thrive here, moose have wandered in from neighboring Vermont and are becoming reestablished. Boreal species attracted to the higher elevation spruce and fir forests include the boreal chickadee, the black-backed and three-toed woodpeckers, the gray jay, and spruce grouse. You can find great expanses of wild, forested mountains often punctuated by ponds, lakes, and rocky river corridors—a place where you can escape for weeks on end or just find a nice quiet campground for a day or two of wildlife watching. In the warmer months you can see peregrine falcons, beavers, waterfowl, wading birds, ospreys, songbirds—many of which prefer a water/wetland habitat. The early morning, dew-drenched, summer landscape echoing with the song of the white-throated

sparrow is archetypical of this area. In the winter snowscape, ravens, crows, and jays frequent the airways while forested, frozen river travelways reveal the drama of predator and prey—the coyotes, fisher, mink, and weasels feed on winter-killed deer, the slides and two-by-two track lines of otter along remote, open-water streams where they feed on fish and crayfish. The Adirondacks are New York's wonderful link with the feeling of the eternal and pristine.

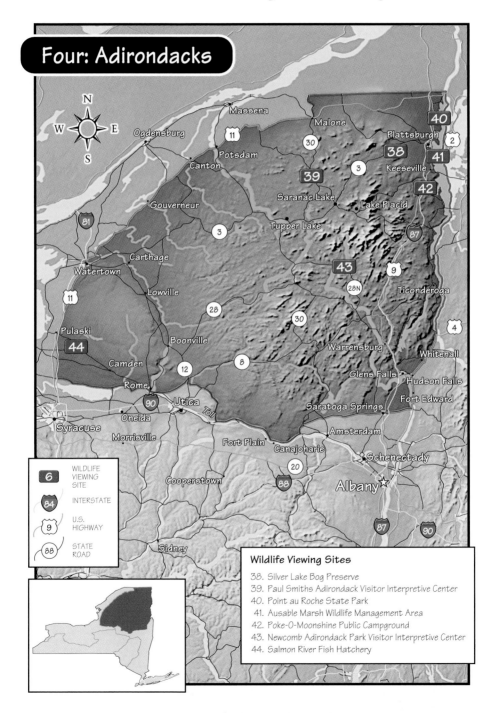

Four: Adirondacks

Wildlife Viewing Sites

38. Silver Lake Bog Preserve
39. Paul Smiths Adirondack Visitor Interpretive Center
40. Point au Roche State Park
41. Ausable Marsh Wildlife Management Area
42. Poke-O-Moonshine Public Campground
43. Newcomb Adirondack Park Visitor Interpretive Center
44. Salmon River Fish Hatchery

38. SILVER LAKE BOG PRESERVE

Description: Silver Lake Bog Preserve contains a wide variety of habitats including a black spruce-tamarack bog, a northern white-cedar swamp, a hemlock–northern hardwood forest and pine ridge. A beautiful new 0.5-mile boardwalk provides easy access to the bog and the trail to the bluffs. At the bluffs, enjoy the view of Silver Lake and Whiteface Mountain. This trail, interpreted by a guide folder from a box at the trailhead, offers a round-trip walk of 2.5 miles. Another Adirondack Nature Conservancy facility worth visiting is the Everton Falls Preserve, protecting 1.5 miles of the St. Regis River. Attractions include 10 miles of canoeable stillwater, a small falls, and a short trail. Contact the Adirondack Nature Conservancy office for directions.

Viewing Information: After the wave of spring migrant warblers pass through in May, some birds remain to nest—the olive-sided flycatcher and Nashville warbler in the bog and the black-throated green warbler in the conifers. Pileated woodpeckers excavate rectangular holes in trees and yellow-bellied sapsuckers leave rows of horizontal holes in hemlock trunks. The bog is excellent habitat for red-backed salamanders. Other herps include spring peepers, wood frogs, and northern leopard frogs. The red eft is the most obvious salamander. Deer and snowshoe hare browse in the bog. Red squirrels and ruffed grouse inhabit the uplands.

Directions: *Silver Lake Bog Preserve is located off the Union Falls Road near Hawkeye. From Exit 34 off the Northway (Interstate 87), take Route 9N west to Ausable Falls. At the blinking red light, turn right and go 0.25 miles to Silver Lake Road. Turn left and travel approximately 15 miles, through the Town of Hawkeye, to the junction with the Union Falls Road (dirt) on the left. The preserve is about 0.3 miles from the Old Hawkeye Road on the right side.*

Ownership: The Adirondack Nature Conservancy 518-576-2082

Size: 61 acres   **Closest Towns:** Ausable Forks and Hawkeye

Warning potential predators of its bad taste with its bright red-orange color, the red eft is the wandering stage of the aquatic red-spotted newt. Newts breed in the shallows of ponds where they feed on almost all types of small animal life, from mosquito larvae and pupae to newly hatched frogs and tadpoles.
CARL E. HEILMAN II

39. PAUL SMITHS ADIRONDACK VISITOR INTERPRETIVE CENTER (VIC)

Description: Paul Smiths VIC introduces visitors to the 6-million-acre Adirondack Forest Preserve. Conifer and northern hardwood forests, brooks, marshes, bogs, and Barnum Pond are connected by 6 miles of trails. Boardwalks and observation platforms enhance the viewing experience. A 17,000-square-foot interpretive building has state-of-the-art exhibits on Adirondack natural history and a 150-seat theater offers three different audio-visual presentations daily.

Viewing Information: After an introduction to the Adirondacks in the interpretive building, visitors are encouraged to follow a trail interpreted by colorful and informative trail signs. Inquire about naturalist-led walks during July and August. Expect to see nesting birds here, such as white-throated sparrow, winter wren and northern junco. Great blue herons and American bittern frequent the marsh. Watch for common loon and river otter in Barnum Pond. Red squirrels and snowshoe hares may be encountered along the trail. Birds of prey at the center include red-tailed and broad-winged hawks, northern harriers, and barred, and saw-whet owls.

Directions: *From Saranac Lake in the Northern Adirondacks, take Route 86 North to Route 30 North and travel one mile to the center entrance.*

Ownership: NYS Adirondack Park Agency 518-327-3000

Size: 3,000 acres   **Closest Town:** Paul Smiths

A canoe trip offers a whole new dimension to wildlife watching. St. Regis Canoe Area is a great place to take advantage of this opportunity. BILL BANASZEWSKI

ADIRONDACKS

40. POINT AU ROCHE STATE PARK

Description: One of the state's newest parks, Point au Roche on the northwestern shore of Lake Champlain is largely undeveloped and natural, with an interesting mix of open and forested land, and marshes and lakeshore edges. A nature center with a self-guiding trail is the focal point of 12 miles of hiking trails. One of the best, a 0.5-mile loop, is wheelchair accessible and hard-topped from the nature center to an embayment of Lake Champlain.

Viewing Information: The abundant wildlife may be comfortably viewed from car or boat as well as on foot. Mallard, black, and wood ducks are abundant, and watch for blue-winged teal and common mergansers. Resident Canada geese nest here. Snow geese, in the fall, and common loons, spring and fall, rest and feed during migration. Killdeer frequent lawns and cattle egret feed on insects in fields near the water. Hawks abound over field and forest and at night, screech, barred, and great horned owls can be heard. Watch for osprey over the lake during the summer. Muskrat, beaver, and otter can be seen in or near the water; white-tailed deer, red fox, and gray fox in fields and forest edges.

Directions: *The park entrance is located approximately 4 miles north of Plattsburgh on Route 9 in northeastern New York. From the Adirondack Northway (Interstate 87), take Exit 40 and follow Route 9 South to the park entrance.*

Ownership: NYS Parks, Recreation and Historic Preservation 518-563-6444

Size: 825 acres   **Closest Town:** Plattsburgh

Our largest land mammal, the moose, wandered into the Adirondacks from Vermont, where breeding has added to a population that now numbers several dozen. BILL BANASZEWSKI

Description: This delta formed from water-borne materials deposited where the Ausable River enters Lake Champlain. A walk here includes spectacular views of historic Valcour Island (just to the north, in Lake Champlain), as well as dramatic views of the Green Mountains across the lake in Vermont. Looking west, visitors can see Whiteface Mountain in the Adirondacks. Wildlife can be viewed from a foot trail that goes through the marsh atop a dike, or from your car on the Ausable Point State Campground Road adjacent to the site. Besides camping, boat access is possible to both the Ausable River and Lake Champlain.

Viewing Information: Over the years, wildlife management practices have enhanced this area for nesting and resting waterfowl. Watch the emergent marsh in the early morning or near dusk for black ducks, blue- and green-winged teals, wood ducks, mallards, hooded mergansers, and common goldeneyes. Canada geese are regular fall migrants. Great blue herons feed on the fish and the green and leopard frogs that you will see leaping into the water. Northern pike and largemouth bass are prized by both anglers and osprey. Osprey use artificial nest platforms placed in the marsh. A winter visit between December and March, after the inland waters have frozen, may reward the viewer with bald eagle sightings. A variety of songbirds including our state bird, the Eastern bluebird, frequent adjacent woodlands, fields and marsh edges. The water and its edges are home to beavers, muskrats, river otters, and mink.

Directions: From the Adirondack Northway (Interstate 87) in northeastern New York south of Plattsburgh, take Exit 35 to Route 442 East to Route 9 North a short distance to the site entrance on the right.

Ownership: NYS Department of Environmental Conservation (518)897-1294

Size: 580 acres   **Closest Town:** Keeseville

Inhabitant of forest treetops, the great-crested flycatcher's presence is most often revealed by its shrill, police-whistle call. Cinnamon wings and tail are this flycatcher's field marks. It feeds on a wide variety of insects, and catches them on the wing.
TOM VEZO

ADIRONDACKS

59

42. POKE-O-MOONSHINE PUBLIC CAMPGROUND

Description: Surrounded by thousands of acres of state land, Poke-O-Moonshine offers a true wilderness experience, highlighted by opportunities to see nesting peregrine falcons. Open for both day use and camping, 25 campsites can each accommodate 30-foot recreational vehicles.

Viewing Information: While a wide variety of mammals and birds may be observed, Poke-O-Moonshine's major attraction is nesting peregrine falcons. The best viewing occurs spring, summer, and fall, in the early morning or evening. A falcon nest is located on the cliff face which may be reached for viewing either along the trail to the top of the mountain or along Route 9 immediately north of the campground. An outstanding view may be enjoyed from the top of the mountain. Watch for broad-winged hawks, turkey vultures, and ravens in flight about the cliff. Ravens are larger than crows and have hoarse, croaking calls. Binoculars will much improve your viewing experience.

Directions: *Poke-O-Moonshine is located south of Plattsburgh northeast of the Adirondacks. Travel 3 miles south on Route 9 from the Adirondack Northway (Interstate 87) Exit 33.*

Ownership: NYS Department of Environmental Conservation 518-897-1200

Size: 275 acres   **Closest Towns:** Keeseville and Willsboro

A threatened bird species in New York, the spruce grouse occurs in only a few lowland spruce stands in the northern Adirondacks. Its diet consists of needles and buds of conifers, and, in summer, berries, seeds, mushrooms, herbaceous leaves, and insects. BILL BANASZEWSKI

43. NEWCOMB ADIRONDACK PARK VISITOR INTERPRETIVE CENTER (VIC)

Description: Newcomb Visitor Interpretive Center provides one of the few boreal forest experiences listed in this viewing guide. Visitors can explore old-growth hemlock, spruce, and northern hardwood forests, wetlands, and lake and river environments on 3.5 miles of bark-surfaced trails.

Viewing Information: Rich Lake, the center's focal point from the spring "ice out" until fall, is home to mallards and black ducks, common loon, common and hooded mergansers, spotted sandpipers, and great blue herons. White-tailed deer, black bear, pine marten, fisher, gray fox, beaver, otter, red squirrel, and snowshoe hare are residents. A 3-mile hike up nearby Goodnow Mountain to its restored fire tower provide some of the best views in the Adirondacks.

Directions: *The center is located in the center of the Adirondack Park. Heading south on the Adirondack Northway (Interstate 87), take Exit 29 Newcomb/North Hudson and then turn left toward Newcomb. Drive 25 miles to the end on Route 28N. Turn right into the town of Newcomb and drive 6 miles to the center entrance on the right. Heading north on the Adirondack Northway (Interstate 87): Take Pottersville Exit 26. Turn left into Pottersville and then right onto Route 9N. At the "Y" in the road, turn left onto Olmstedville/Minerva Road until it ends on Route 28N. Turn right onto 28N and drive 25 miles to the Town of Newcomb. Then drive 6 miles to the center entrance on the right.*

Ownership: NYS Adirondack Park Agency 518-582-2000

Size: 365 acres   **Closest Town:** Newcomb

44. SALMON RIVER FISH HATCHERY

Description: Among the most modern hatcheries in North America, this facility raises four million coho salmon, chinook salmon, steelhead, Atlantic salmon, and brown trout. Inside, visitors can see fascinating displays and exhibits, watch a video, and see the giant fish tanks.

Viewing Information: The best times to visit the hatchery are during the spawning season when fish are jumping up the ladder, eggs are being harvested, and fish are being tagged. The spawning season is in October for salmon and late March to early April for steelhead.

Directions: *On Interstate 81 north of Syracuse, take Exit 36 and then drive 7-8 miles east on Route 13 to Altmar. Turn left onto County Route 22 North. Go straight through the first intersection. The hatchery is 0.5 miles on the left.*

Ownership: NYS Department of Environmental Conservation 315-298-5051

Size: 430 acres   **Closest Town:** Altmar

ADIRONDACKS

REGION FIVE: HUDSON VALLEY

Extending north from New York City on both sides of the Hudson River to Albany, this ecozone is rich in both cultural and natural history. Agricultural land, parks and the river itself all add to this zone's diversity. Migrating waterfowl form large "rafts" in spring and autumn, either in protected bays of the river or out in the main channel. Many sections of the river lend themselves to canoe trips. Day trips are especially popular near the fall and spring equinoxes, when large flocks of migrating songbirds going to roost in riverside swamps provide a wondrous spectacle. Walking the shoreline is also a great way to see wildlife in this sharply contrasting landscape. Riverside agricultural fields host large flocks of Canada and snow geese where corn has been late harvested. Bald eagles winter at a few places along the Hudson to the south. To the north in late November, following the opening of the locks for winter, the Mohawk River's water level drops considerably, affording great expanses of open shoreline increasing access to see waterfowl and gulls, as well as the occasional

migrating bald eagle. In winter, northern agricultural lands often host concentrations of hawks and owls (some quite rare such as the snowy owl, hawk owl, and golden eagle), as well as flocks of geese, which roost on open water lakes and feed on snow-free farm fields. The contrast of agricultural lands and mountain peaks in this zone is quite unique for New York and exceptionally pleasing to see.

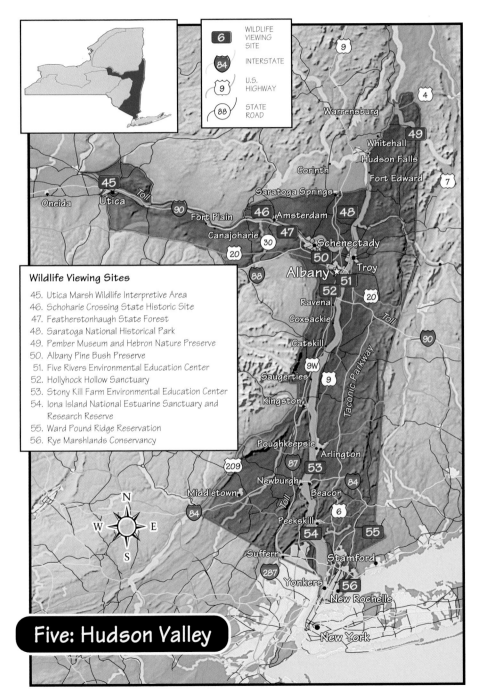

WILDLIFE VIEWING SITE

INTERSTATE

U.S. HIGHWAY

STATE ROAD

Wildlife Viewing Sites

45. Utica Marsh Wildlife Interpretive Area
46. Schoharie Crossing State Historic Site
47. Featherstonhaugh State Forest
48. Saratoga National Historical Park
49. Pember Museum and Hebron Nature Preserve
50. Albany Pine Bush Preserve
51. Five Rivers Environmental Education Center
52. Hollyhock Hollow Sanctuary
53. Stony Kill Farm Environmental Education Center
54. Iona Island National Estuarine Sanctuary and Research Reserve
55. Ward Pound Ridge Reservation
56. Rye Marshlands Conservancy

Five: Hudson Valley

45. UTICA MARSH WILDLIFE INTERPRETIVE AREA

Description: Utica Marsh is an urban wildlife sanctuary. With two observation towers, trails throughout (some accommodating persons with disabilities), boat launch sites on both the Mohawk River and Barge Canal, and a paved bike trail along the canal, this wetland is very accessible.

Viewing Information: Expect to see or find signs of a number of different marsh dwellers. An early spring visit at dusk might reward you with the courtship display of the American woodcock. Expect to hear the familiar conk-a-ree of the red-winged blackbird all along the trail. Other common marsh birds include song and swamp sparrows, yellow warbler and yellowthroat, and marsh wren. Watch for frogs, turtles, and garter snakes.

Directions: *From Utica in east-central New York, take Route 5A West (Oriskany Boulevard), to a right onto Barnes Avenue site parking area.*

Ownership: NYS Department of Environmental Conservation (brochure available) 315-793-2554

Size: 213 acres   **Closest Town:** Utica

46. SCHOHARIE CROSSING STATE HISTORIC SITE

Description: This state historic site interprets the history of the Erie Canal and its impact on the growth of New York State and the nation. With 2.5 miles of Mohawk River access and both the original and enlarged Erie Canals, this site hosts a variety of wildlife.

Viewing Information: From the visitor center, a towpath follows the canal for 2.5 miles, while a shorter loop trail takes walkers to two locks. Both of these trails offer excellent viewing opportunities. Canada geese use the creek and the river, while mallards, common mergansers, and blue-winged teal also feed in the canals. Killdeer use the fields and woodchucks den at the edge of woods. Both muskrat and beaver can be seen. Ask at the visitor center for a self-guiding nature tour brochure.

Directions: *From the east, take the New York State Thruway (Interstate 90), Exit 27 (Amsterdam), and turn right onto Route 30 North and then take an immediate right onto the Route 5S ramp. Turn left onto Route 5S and go to Fort Hunter. Turn right onto Main Street and then left onto Railroad Street. The visitor center is on the right. From the west, take the New York State Thruway Exit 28 (Fultonville). Turn right onto Riverside Drive. At the T intersection, turn left onto Route 5S to Fort Hunter and then turn left onto Main Street and follow the directions above.*

Ownership: NYS Parks, Recreation and Historic Preservation 518-829-7516

Size: 245 acres   **Closest Town:** Fort Hunter

47. FEATHERSTONHAUGH STATE FOREST

Description: Featherstonhaugh contains a wide variety of habitat—from forest upland to shrubland to wooded red maple swamp to open water with associated bog wetland. As a result, the site supports many wildlife species.

Viewing Information: Walk from the parking area down to the lake for great views from the dock overlook. Visitors are welcome to carry in a canoe or kayak to explore the lake and the lakeside bog mat on the other side. The bog contains black spruce, insectivorous sundews, and pitcher plants. A special trip to the lake in spring or fall gives visitors the chance to see the resting and feeding migrating waterfowl. Watch for Canada geese and the following ducks: mallards, black, wood, and ring-necked ducks (large flocks of the latter), and common and hooded mergansers. Other birds attracted to the water include great blue and green herons, horned grebe, belted kingfisher, and osprey. You are also very likely to see beaver and muskrat—or their signs. Pick up a brochure with map to find the location of upland trails perfect for birding, hiking, or cross-country skiing in winter. As you explore, watch and listen for signs of deer, river otter, woodcock, ruffed grouse, and wild turkey.

Directions: *From Schenectady and Rotterdam in the Capital district, take Route 159 West to a left onto Lake Road. Then take a diagonal right onto graveled Judith Lane and proceed to the main parking area on the right.*

Ownership: NYS Department of Environmental Conservation 518-357-2066

Size: 697 acres   **Closest Towns:** Mariaville and Duanesburg

From unusual ice meadows (pictured here) to fresh and brackish marshes to flood plain forests, the Hudson River's shores offer a wide variety of wildlife species and scenic beauty. GERARD LEMMO

48. SARATOGA NATIONAL HISTORICAL PARK

Description: Saratoga is the site of one of the most decisive battles of the Revolutionary War, fought in 1777. Today, the park is a premier wildlife-viewing area. The 9-mile tour road is accessible by both car and bicycle. There are ten pulloffs with signs offering historic interpretation, which also offer excellent wildlife watching. Walking, horse, and cross-country ski trails are also available for visitors.

Viewing Information: Shortly after dawn and at dusk are prime viewing times. Hundreds of acres along the road are kept open and afford excellent opportunities to see white-tailed deer, woodchuck, wild turkey, American goldfinch, nesting bobolink, and Eastern bluebird. Mallard, merganser, wood duck, and Canada geese grace the adjacent Hudson River. Watch for beaver, muskrat, and great blue heron in the water. Look overhead for more than six species of birds of prey. Watch and listen for owls in the evening. Serious birders visit the park in hopes of seeing the uncommon Henslow's sparrow. While looking for it in old fields, one may encounter savannah and grasshopper sparrows and Eastern meadowlarks.

Directions: *From Schuylerville, north of Albany, drive 7 miles south on Route 4 to the park entrance on the right. From the Adirondack Northway (Interstate 87), take Exit 12 and follow signs for Saratoga National Historical Park.*

Ownership: National Park Service 518-664-9821

Size: 3,200 acres   **Closest Town:** Stillwater

The Eastern garter snake, one of our most abundant snakes, thrives on our even more abundant earthworms, along with frogs, toads, salamanders, and insects. In late summer, 12–70 young are live born. The garter snake is not poisonous, but it does exude a disagreeable musk from its glands when picked up. THOMAS D. LINDSAY

Description: The small Washington County village of Granville has one of the finest Victorian-era natural history collections in the state. Row upon row of antique glass cases house specimens of nearly every species of North American bird and mammal, plus many from around the world. Shells, butterflies and moths, and plant herbarium sheets round out this most impressive Pember Museum of Natural History, which opened in 1909. A visit to the Hebron Nature Preserve, located 8 miles south of Granville, complements the museum visit with seven nature trails through deciduous and coniferous woods, past stream edges, alder thickets and marshy ponds, over an esker, and up a hemlock hillside. An observation deck provides a panoramic view of the preserve, and a restored one-room schoolhouse on Route 22 offers an orientation site and nature center for visiting school groups.

Viewing Information: The rich variety of wildlife reflects the preserve's ecological diversity. Red squirrels, chickadees, woodpeckers, and nuthatches are among the most obvious conifer-stand inhabitants. Great horned owls and deer are residents here, and ruffed grouse are sometimes scared up from the trail. Watch for porcupine in the trees and raccoons feeding at the water's edge at dusk. You will find frogs and spotted newt salamanders in the marsh shallows. Muskrat and beaver lodges reveal their makers' presence. Check the tops of beaver dams and muskrat lodges with binoculars; fish scales and bones are a sure sign of otter. Mallards, teals, and wood ducks are the most common waterfowl. Listen for red-winged blackbirds' *conk-a-ree* and yellowthroats' *witchery-witch* in the alder thicket. Woodland wildflowers in spring and field flowers in summer attract both humans and butterflies. An excellent trail map helps visitors choose the trails and terrain they wish to walk.

Directions: *From the Adirondack Northway (Interstate 87), north of Albany, take the Fort Ann Exit 20 and then travel 30 miles east on Route 149 to Granville where the museum is in the center of the village at 33 West Main Street. To get to the nature preserve, go 8 miles south of Granville on Route 22 to the preserve on the right.*

Ownership: Pember Library and Museum of Natural History 518-642-1515

Size: 125 acres   **Closest Town:** Granville

HUDSON VALLEY

The Karner blue butterfly is one of only two endangered insect species in New York. This small butterfly, whose caterpillar feeds exclusively on wild blue lupine leaves, lives only in a few locations, such as the pine bush of Albany and Saratoga counties.

50. ALBANY PINE BUSH PRESERVE

Description: The Albany Pine Bush Preserve contains the best remaining example of an inland pine-barrens ecosystem in the northeastern United States. Of global ecological significance, this diverse ecosystem includes a variety of habitats, including fire-dependent, pitch pine–scrub oak barrens, vernal ponds, red maple hardwood swamps, hardwood forests, and deep ravines. Without fires, fire-dependent communities in time would revert to the prevailing surrounding deciduous forest. An extensive trail system provides access for horseback riding, hiking, and cross-country skiing.

Viewing Information: Most appealing for its unusual vegetation and gently rolling sand dunes, the Pine Bush differs from the more common deciduous forests and hills found throughout New York and New England. The Pine Bush supports 16 rare species, two rare natural communities, and hundreds of other more common, but no less worthy species. One of the most famous is the federally listed endangered Karner blue butterfly. Wildlife commonly encountered include white-tailed deer, cottontail rabbits, foxes, and coyotes. The Eastern spadefoot (a toad), hognose snake, and (rarely) spotted turtle are among the reptiles and amphibians that can be observed in the warmer months. Birds frequently observed in the Pine Bush include blue jays, rufous-sided towhee, American woodcock, American bittern, great blue heron, great horned owl, and red-tailed hawk. The blue jay and rufous-sided towhee are the most common. You are likely to see hawks, most notably the red-tailed soaring overhead. Watch for recent evidence of control burns along the trial. Fire management is used to maintain the flora and fauna of the Pine Bush.

Directions: *From Albany, take Interstate 90 west to the Adirondack Northway (Interstate 87). Travel north 1.2 miles to Exit 2W. Follow Central Avenue (Route 5) west 2.4 miles to a left turn onto New Karner Road (Route 155) for 1.7 miles. Park on the left side of New Karner road along the dirt road located in grassy margin near trail head marked by routed sign.*

Ownership: Albany Pine Bush Commission 518-464-6496

Size: 2,300 acres   **Closest Town:** Albany

In the Albany Pine Bush, dominant scarlet oaks and pitch pine pale by comparison with the blaze of red of heath family shrubs turning in the fall: huckleberry, blueberry, and deerberry. FRANK KNIGHT

68

Description: At the center, more than 5 miles of walking and cross-country ski trails lead wildlife viewers through fields, orchards, forests, and successional areas regrowing to scrub and forest, along streams, through marshes, and around ponds. Two short, level trails close to parking and the interpretive building are wheelchair accessible. Picnic tables and shelters, also accessible to persons with disabilities, entice visitors to bring a lunch. Inside, interactive exhibits that will captivate the entire family interpret the natural history of the site. The building is open all year.

Viewing Information: Five Rivers' varied habitats make the center a bird paradise with more than 200 species recorded. Stop in at the interpretive building for a bird checklist and note the "Bird Watcher's Board" listing the current year's first arrival dates and recent sightings of special interest. Outside watch for the state bird, the Eastern bluebird, around nest boxes or in the old fields. Tree swallows, bobolinks, robins, redstarts, and pileated woodpeckers are also seen. Depending on the season, expect to see Canada geese nesting, leading young on a pond, or feeding them in a field. The ponds are also home to black and wood ducks, mallards, bitterns, muskrats, beavers, painted and snapping turtles, salamanders, spring peepers, bullfrogs, and wood frogs. Bass, bullhead, and sunfish are easily seen along the edges of the shallow ponds in the spring. Watch for red-tailed hawks soaring overhead and be alert for turkey signs or sightings. Walk the North Loop Trail in the morning or evening and you are likely to see white-tailed deer. Cross-country skiers regularly hear screech-owls and great horned owls in January at dusk along the Vlomankill Trail.

Directions: *From downtown Albany, take Route 443, Delaware Avenue south through Delmar 1.3 miles beyond the Route 52 intersection to a right turn onto Orchard Street. Follow signs to Game Farm Road and the center. From the New York State Thruway (Interstate 87), take Exit 23 to Route 9W South to Route 32 to Delmar. From Route 32, turn right onto Route 443 and proceed as above.*

Ownership: NYS Department of Environmental Conservation 518-475-0291

Size: 328 acres   **Closest Towns:** Delmar and Albany

HUDSON VALLEY

The yellow warbler's "sweet, sweet, sweet, I am so sweet" call helps locate this bird among willows and alders along streams and ponds. Their nests frequently parasitized by cowbirds, yellow warblers often build another nest covering the first and lay another clutch.
ARTHUR MORRIS

52. HOLLYHOCK HOLLOW SANCTUARY

Description: Hollyhock Hollow, located in southern Albany County, is noted for its variety and abundance of wildflowers. Eight trails provide visitors with easy access to all parts of this mostly wooded refuge. A trail map is available and two of the trails have interpretive booklets to guide the visitor. Designed to provide ideas for attracting wildlife to your property, The Back Yard Habitat Trail has separate butterfly, hummingbird, and songbird gardens. A staffed office is open weekdays all year.

Viewing Information: More than 80 species of birds have been seen at Hollyhock Hollow and about 60 of them nest there. A checklist is available in the trail kiosk. Ducks are attracted to the creek and pond. The greatest variety of songbirds can be seen during the spring migration in May. Hummingbirds grace the gardens during spring and summer. Old stone walls along the wooded trails are home to a number of chipmunks. Flying squirrels use nest boxes in the garden area and become active at dusk. Frogs and turtles can be seen in the small pond. Butterflies are attracted to the flowers in the gardens.

Directions: *The sanctuary is located 15 miles south of Albany. Take Interstate 787 South from Albany to its end and turn right onto Route 9W South. Travel one mile to Route 32 South. (Route 9W South can also be accessed here from Exit 23 of the New York State Thruway (Interstate 87)). In the village of Feura Bush, turn left onto Route 102, Old Quarry Road. Drive 3 miles to the sign for the sanctuary at Rarick Road. Turn right onto Rarick Road and go a short ways to the parking lot.*

Ownership: Audubon Society of New York State 518-767-9051

Size: 138 acres   **Closest Town:** Feura Bush

Look for wood frogs on the forest floor, where they feed on insects and other small animals. At spring breeding ponds, the males' hoarse clacking sounds like the quack of a duck. DAVE SPIER

53. STONY KILL FARM ENVIRONMENTAL EDUCATION CENTER

Description: A working farm since the late 1600s, Stony Kill today helps city and suburb residents understand farming's important role in land conservation and stewardship. Owned and operated by the NYS Department of Environmental Conservation, the center demonstrates agricultural practices, including raising field crops and livestock, which are interpreted in school and public programming. Exceptionally large and very old trees are scattered throughout the forest and lawns. Several miles of walking and cross-country ski trails traverse fields, marshes, swamps, forests, and pond edges. All of the buildings, including the barns and the 1840 Manor House Interpretive Building are on the National Register of Historic Places.

Viewing Information: Woodchucks can be seen keeping vigil on mounds beside their den holes in pastures. Visitors occasionally see them hunted and taken by coyotes. White-tailed deer, foxes, raccoons, skunks, cottontail rabbits, and squirrels are frequently seen on trails. Resident red-tailed hawks can be seen circling overhead or perched quietly in a tree. Woodcocks perform their courtship rituals in overgrown fields beginning in April. Ducks and geese are attracted to the ponds, and songbirds migrate through and nest in the spring. The best birding occurs on forest edges. During the colder months, feeder birds can be watched from the Manor House library. Community garden plots are maintained near the barn each summer. Weed seeds here attract large numbers of sparrows and other winter birds all winter. Many of Stony Kill's wildlife viewings are part of the center's public programming. Phone the center at the number below for a quarterly program schedule.

Directions: The center is located 2.5 miles north on Route 9D from Interstate 84 and the Newburgh-Beacon Bridge south of Poughkeepsie in the Hudson Valley. Access Interstate 84 from the New York State Thruway (Interstate 87), Exit 17 (east of the Hudson River), or from the Taconic Parkway (west of the Hudson River).

Ownership: NYS Department of Environmental Conservation 914-831-8780

Size: 457 acres   **Closest Town:** Wappingers Falls

HUDSON VALLEY

Many people begin their wildlife watching at home by attracting birds with sunflower seeds and suet feeders, or by planting colorful flowers to lure butterflies and hummingbirds.

54. IONA ISLAND NATIONAL ESTUARINE SANCTUARY AND RESEARCH RESERVE

Description: Iona Island is one of four National Estuarine Research Reserves on the Hudson River (the others are Piermont Marsh, Tivoli Bays, and Stockport Flats). It is a spectacular setting at the southern gate of the Hudson Highlands. Steep wooded slopes plunging into the narrow Hudson and tidal wetlands surround the west side of a rocky island. Food, water, and toilets are available at nearby Bear Mountain State Park.

Viewing Information: The 6,000-year-old tidal marsh of 200 acres is home to mute swans, Canada geese, and mallards. Smaller birds include the swamp sparrow, marsh wren, willow flycatcher, yellow throat, and least bittern. Deer are often visible in the marsh and muskrats in the tidal creeks. Estuarine animals include killifish, grass shrimp, barnacles, blue crabs, and fiddler crabs. Young striped bass feed in the marsh creeks. The highlight of a winter visit is seeing bald eagles roosting on the island (best viewing is from the pulloff on Route 6/202 on the opposite side of the river). On-site viewing is best from the marsh edge along the road and the railroad causeway. The steep sloped knolls and Iona Island east of the railroad are off limits.

Directions: *From the New York State Thruway (Interstate 87), north of New York City, take Exit 16 to Route 6E to the Bear Mountain Bridge traffic circle. Go south on Route 9W 1.5 miles and turn left onto the causeway through the marsh to the parking area just west of the railroad tracks.*

Ownership: Palisades Interstate Park Commission 914-786-2701

Size: 550 acres   **Closest Town:** Bear Mountain

Nestled between bold promontories of the Hudson Highlands, Iona Island is one of the few sites on the Hudson where one can walk dryshod on a quiet road across the middle of a major marsh. Iona Marsh is an ecological history book which tells the story of 6,000 years of marsh development, vegetation change, wildlife occupation, and use by Indians and the United States Navy.
HARDIE TRUESDALE

55. WARD POUND RIDGE RESERVATION

Description: Ward Pound Ridge is Westchester County's largest park with beautiful fields, woodlands, picnic and recreation areas, and an extensive 50-mile trail system through diverse wildlife viewing areas and along a river.

Viewing Information: Begin your tour at the historic Trailside Museum to enjoy the interpretive exhibits and learn about self-guided and guided trail options. Eighty-five bird species nest at Pound Ridge including the Eastern bluebird. Sixty bluebird boxes help provide easy viewing. Common mammals include white-tailed deer, cottontail rabbits, gray squirrels, red fox, muskrats, and river otters. Park staff have identified 49 species of butterflies and more than 500 species of wildflowers. Wet areas are home to eight species of salamanders and six species of frogs. Watch in the river for brown and brook trout, dace, and smallmouth bass.

Directions: *From Interstate 684 in northern Westchester County north of New York City, take Exit 6 East 3.8 miles to the park entrance.*

Ownership: Westchester County 914-763-3993

Size: 4,700 acres   **Closest Town:** Cross River

56. RYE MARSHLANDS CONSERVANCY

Description: Part of the National Heritage Site containing the John Jay property and cemetery, Rye Marshlands has an interesting mix of broad, open fields, maturing woodlands, and a tidal saltmarsh on Long Island Sound. A small interpretive building next to the parking lot orients the visitor and offers exhibits and self-guided trail guides.

Viewing Information: While Marshlands attracts many species of upland mammals and birds, the real attraction here is the saltmarsh. Plan to extend your visit to enjoy the changes as the tide comes in or goes out. Fiddler and hermit crabs, crustaceans, and periwinkle snails are a few of the many creatures to be seen in or near the shallow water. Check with the naturalist about the horseshoe crab egg-laying in the spring and plan to return then for a fascinating interpretive program. Water birds are a special treat. Great blue herons, black-crowned night herons, glossy ibis, godwits, curlews, and oystercatchers may all be seen.

Directions: *Rye is located off Interstate 95 on Long Island Sound north of New York City. Take Route 1 less than one mile south of Rye's business district to the signed entrance on left.*

Ownership: Westchester County 914-835-4466

Size: 32 acres   **Closest Town:** Rye

REGION SIX: NEW YORK CITY

It may seem surprising, but some of the state's best wildlife viewing actually occurs within New York City limits. On the shores of the Atlantic Ocean and divided by the Hudson, Harlem, and East rivers, much of New York City is bordered by seashore, tidal estuaries, and marshes. These habitats, along with the thousands of acres of forests and meadows in the city's parks, attract and sustain a rich diversity of both seasonal and permanent wildlife species.

The most conspicuous wildlife in New York City are the birds. Located on the Atlantic Flyway, one of the nation's premier migration routes, the city is visited by waves of songbirds each spring and fall. To the delight of birders, many of these migrants stop to rest and feed in the city's parks before continuing on their journeys. The Ramble in Central Park attracts so many different songbirds to such a concentrated area that it has earned a reputation for being one of the Northeast's best birding spots.

An array of waterfowl, birds of prey, and shorebirds are also seen in, and above, New York City. Red-tailed hawks are seen nesting on apartment buildings and flying over city parks every day searching for prey. Peregrine falcons find ample food in the city, mostly in the form of pigeons, and nest on major suspension bridges which substitute for the birds' natural cliff top aeries. Each fall as many as 14 other species of raptors, such as bald and golden eagles, sharp-shinned, Cooper's, and broad-winged hawks, turkey vultures, and

ospreys, are spotted as they migrate over New York City. Many species of owls can be found in city parks during the winter months. Piping plovers and least terns, both of which are New York state-listed endangered species, nest on a small stretch of Rockaway Beach, Queens.

Coyotes, turkeys, deer, and foxes are seen increasingly in the city's remnant forests. More than 50 species of butterflies are identified each year in meadows throughout the city. Bullfrogs, spring peepers, spotted salamanders, and painted turtles are

Nearly eliminated as a breeding bird in the northeast by DDT, the peregrine falcon has been reestablished and is doing well. In New York City, it nests on suspension bridges and feeds on pigeons. MICHAEL FELLER

abundant, if elusive, in the city's wetlands. Raccoons, opossums, and skunks scavenge the city's parks by night, chipmunks and squirrels scamper in the brush by day. Great spring runs of shad, striped bass, and sturgeon rush up the Hudson River to breed. So take your binoculars and spend the day discovering for yourself the surprising diversity of wildlife that New York City has to offer.

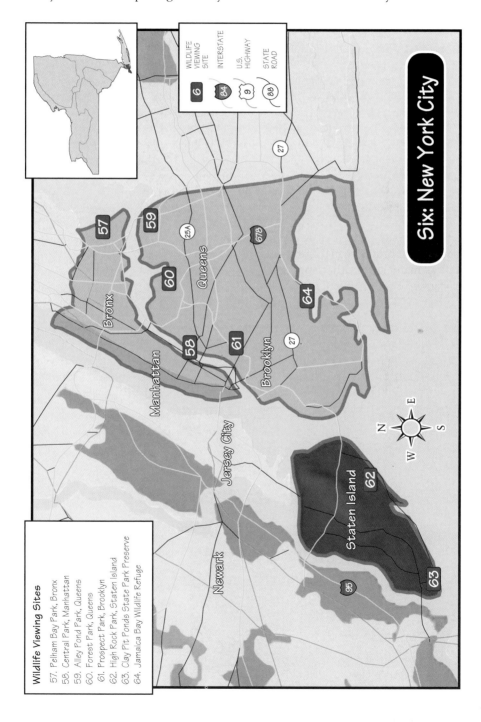

Six: New York City

Wildlife Viewing Sites

57. Pelham Bay Park, Bronx
58. Central Park, Manhattan
59. Alley Pond Park, Queens
60. Forest Park, Queens
61. Prospect Park, Brooklyn
62. High Rock Park, Staten Island
63. Clay Pit Ponds State Park Preserve
64. Jamaica Bay Wildlife Refuge

Description: Pelham Bay Park is not only New York City's largest park, it is probably its most ecologically diverse, a real country haven on the city's edge. Habitats include rocky seashore, salt marsh, meadows, and a mature natural forest. All teem with wildlife year-round. The Urban Park Rangers provide free school programs and public tours in Pelham Bay Park throughout the year.

Viewing Information: Information and written materials from the Pelham Bay Environmental Center on the boardwalk at Orchard Beach's north end will enrich visitor viewing experiences. Start by using the guide booklet and take the nearby Kazimiroff Nature Trail through the 189-acre Hunter Island forest (now connected to the mainland), which starts and ends at the salt marsh and meadow. This forest at Pelham Bay is one of New York City's best owl haunts. Droppings, regurgitated owl pellets, and mobbing jays and crows often aid viewers in seeing great horned, Eastern screech, Northern saw-whet, long-eared, and barred owls. This forest is also home to wild turkey and passing deer and coyotes. Check open areas during the winter along Orchard Beach and around its parking lot for snowy owls visiting from the far North. Another common bird in the spring is the well-camouflaged American woodcock. In April and May, listen at dusk on the 25-acre meadow for the male's nasal peent and watch its spectacular aerobatic courtship flights. The Thomas Pell Wildlife Refuge, near the park's western boundary, is a salt marsh dotted by forested rock outcrops. In the marsh see green and great blue herons and great and snowy egrets. Ring-necked pheasants are sometimes seen on the marsh edges.

Directions: *From New York City, take the IRT Lexington Avenue #6 subway train to Pelham Bay Park station. Or during the summer, take the #12 bus to Orchard Beach. By car, north of the City, take either the New England Thruway to the Orchard Beach exit, or the Hutchinson River Parkway to the City Island/Orchard Beach exit. Follow the signs to Orchard Beach. Get information at the Pelham Bay Environmental Center at the north end of the beach.*

Ownership: City of New York Department of Parks and Recreation. Urban Park Rangers 1-800-201-PARK

Size: 2,764 acres   **Closest Towns:** City Island and Orchard Beach

The saw-whet owl, our smallest owl, becomes vocal in late winter and early spring, uttering calls in groups of three that sound like the filing of a saw. They hunt and roost close to the ground in dense, low, wet evergreen forests.
TOM VEZO

58. CENTRAL PARK, MANHATTAN

Description: Central Park's wonderfully diverse ecosystem, with freshwater ponds, lakes, meadows, and dense forest, attracts both wildlife and wildlife watchers. An island of green surrounded by city, Central Park attracts many migrating birds that stop to rest and feed here. The Urban Park Rangers provide school programs and free public tours of Central Park.

Viewing Information: Harlem Meer, a lake in the northeast corner, attracts mallards and black ducks, Canada geese, and wading birds such as the great blue heron and black-crowned night heron. Several resident double-crested cormorants are often seen diving for fish. The wooded 38-acre Ramble in the center of the park offers the best birding. Enthusiastic birders and rangers at the Belvedere Castle are on hand daily to share their knowledge. From early September to early December, the best viewing is from the steps and terrace of Belvedere Castle facing north. Just to the north, the large reservoir provides the best winter duck viewing in and around Manhattan. Finally, the beautiful Conservatory Garden is an excellent place to see butterflies, hummingbirds, and warblers in the spring and early summer.

Directions: *The park is bordered on the north by Central Park North (110th St.) and Central Park South on the south (59th St.). Adjacent Central Park West and Fifth Avenue are accessible by bus, subway, taxi, car and on foot. Phone for a Central Park conservancy map and guide brochure.*

Ownership: City of New York Department of Parks and Recreation. Belvedere Castle 212-772-0210. Urban Park Rangers 1-800-201-PARK

Size: 843 acres   **Closest Town:** Manhattan

Central Park offers food and rest for migrating birds and a treat for birders of all ages. ARTHUR MORRIS

Description: The largest and most diverse of Queens' natural parklands, Alley Pond Park is a varied ecosystem which consists of beech forest, salt marsh, upland meadow, and freshwater wetlands. Alley Pond Park stretches from Little Neck Bay south to Union Turnpike. The Urban Park Rangers give free school programs and public tours in Alley Pond Park throughout the year.

Viewing Information: Alley Pond Park's glacial kettle ponds teem with insects and such unusual city dwellers as spotted salamanders, bullfrogs, spring peepers, and Fowler's toads. Ring-necked pheasant, bobwhite quail, and many smaller birds feed on the abundant insects and seeds. In fact, Alley Pond Park has the greatest insect diversity in New York City. Muskrats thrive on the aquatic vegetation. Predators include red-tailed, broad-winged, and Cooper's hawks, and the red fox.

Directions: *To reach the Alley wetlands in New York City's northeastern Queens County, take the IRT Flushing Line subway train #7 to Main Street and then the #12 bus to Northern Boulevard. By car, take the Long Island Expressway (Interstate 495) to Douglaston Parkway, north to a left onto Northern Boulevard and then three blocks to the park. Inquire at the phone number below for separate directions to Alley Pond Park's upland forest.*

Ownership: City of New York Department of Parks and Recreation. Urban Park Rangers 1-800-201-PARK

Size: 654 acres   **Closest Town:** Douglaston

A popular game bird upstate, the ring-necked pheasant graces several city parks where it nests in fields and feeds on weeds seeds, and insects. TOM VEZO

Description: Forest Park, Queens' third largest, sits on an ancient glacial ridge near the center of the borough. Its high rocky terrain, ill-suited to either agriculture or cityscaping, has ensured its preservation as parkland. Bisected by Woodhaven Boulevard, the western half supports a golf course, playgrounds, baseball diamonds, and athletic courts. In the eastern half, three color-coded nature trails and bridle paths meander through such forested sections as the Gully, the Northern Forest, and the Pine Grove. This forested ridge is a haven for both resident and migrating wildlife. The Urban Park Rangers provide free school programs and public tours in Forest Park throughout the year.

Viewing Information: Forest Park contains the largest continuous oak forest in Queens. With trees more than 150 years old, the forest has three distinct layers: the forest floor, the understory, and the tree canopy. On the forest floor, white-footed mice and chipmunks search out seeds and berries while secretive short-tail shrews voraciously eat earthworms, insects, and even mice. In the understory thick with vines, shrubs, and small trees, watch for songbirds and gray squirrels. Each spring, the forest canopy is a green magnet for about 100 species of migrating birds that pause here to rest and feed on their way to nesting sites further north. In the late fall, especially on days with northwest winds, watch broad-winged, red-tailed, sharp-shinned, and other majestic hawks migrating along the park's ridge. Some red-tailed hawks overwinter in the city's parks. Forest Park is also home to a nesting pair of great horned owls.

Directions: *In New York City, take the J subway train to Woodhaven Boulevard and Jamaica Avenue or 102nd Street. Transfer to the Q11 bus which runs north-south along Woodhaven/Cross Bay Boulevard between Horace Harding Expressway and Jamaica Bay. Take the Q11 to Forest Park Drive. By car, take the Van Wyck Expressway south to the Union Turnpike exit. Take a left on Markwood Place/Park Lane and enter the park drive near the Overlook.*

Ownership: City of New York Department of Parks and Recreation. Urban Park Rangers 1-800-201-PARK

Size: 538 acres   **Closest Town:** Woodhaven, Queens

The gray squirrel is probably New York's most seen and enjoyed wildlife species. Nesting in tree cavities or in leaf nests, these rodents feed on leaf buds, seeds, and nuts. They bury large numbers of acorns in the fall, which they dig up through the winter. GERARD LEMMO

NEW YORK CITY

61. PROSPECT PARK, BROOKLYN

Description: Wildlife viewing is just one of many cultural and recreational opportunities available in Prospect Park. The park is home to the Brooklyn Museum, Ingerson Library, the Zoo, Botanical Garden, and two classic buildings—the Litchfield Villa and the Picnic House. Brooklyn is the least forested of the city's five boroughs, and nearly all of its forest is in Prospect Park. In two forested areas, the Midwood and the Ravine, a stream and several lakes combine to provide habitat for a large variety of terrestrial and aquatic wildlife. Designed by Frederick Law Olmsted and Calvert Vaux, the park is undergoing a comprehensive face-lift. The entire 25-year forest rehabilitation can be viewed as a work in progress. The Urban Park Rangers provide free school programs and public tours in Prospect Park throughout the year.

Viewing Information: A number of marked nature trails, some with no stairs and easy wheelchair access, lead visitors through the forests and past the lakes. An extensive internal roadway is also very helpful in this large park. Gray squirrels and the only remaining population of chipmunks in Brooklyn are the most obvious mammals in the wooded areas. More than 100 species of birds have been seen in the park, many of them warblers and other songbirds passing through during the spring migration in May. Red-bellied, hairy, and downy woodpeckers are among the more than 30 bird species that nest here. The lake and its wetlands are home to mute swans and such ducks as wigeon, ruddy, pintail, teal, and gadwall. Great blue and green herons, great and snowy egrets, and black-crowned night heron search out frogs and fish. Green frogs leap into the shallow water while snapping turtles emerge in spring to lay eggs. Painted turtles and red-eared sliders bask atop logs in the sun.

Directions: *By subway, take the F train to Seventh Avenue Station, exit at 8th Ave. (front of train). At 8th Ave. and 9th St., walk up 9th to the park one avenue away. Turn left onto Prospect Park West and enter the park at 5th St. Or take the D,Q,S train to Prospect Park Station. Enter the park at Ocean and Parkside Avenues. Buses 16, 41, 43, 48, 68, 69, 71 access the park. By car, from the Brooklyn Bridge, stay on bridge through first traffic light onto Adam St. which becomes Boerum Place. Turn left onto Atlantic Ave. at Mobil Station. At the YWCA, turn right onto 3rd Ave. and then left onto Union St. through the traffic circle at Grand Army Plaza and bear right onto Flatbush Ave. to a right turn onto Ocean Ave. Enter the park at Ocean and Parkside Avenues. Park at the Wollman Rink lot on the left. From the Verrazano Bridge, take the Brooklyn-Queens Expressway East (Interstate 278). Exit at 38th St. and turn left onto 4th Ave. Turn right onto Union Street and follow directions above.*

Ownership: City of New York Department of Parks and Recreation. Urban Park Rangers 1-800-201-PARK

Size: 526 acres   **Closest Town:** Brooklyn

Description: High Rock Park is part of the Greenbelt, a 2,500-acre chain of nine natural areas on Staten Island connected by 35 miles of walking trails. Comprising glacial ponds, upland meadows, conifer, gum, and oak forests, and lowlands of cattail marsh and red maple swamps, the Greenbelt is an excellent wildlife viewing site. The Nature Center in High Rock Park, run by the New York City Urban Park Rangers, offers free school programs, workshops, exhibits, and trail maps. It is the perfect starting point for a short or long hike.

Viewing Information: On almost any walk along a forest trail, you can expect to see gray squirrels and chipmunks. Wood thrush, rufous-sided towhee, and red-bellied woodpecker nest in the oak forests. Red-tailed hawks and great horned owls are important predators. Black-capped chickadees, tufted titmice, and Northern flickers make their homes in the red maple swamps. Visit in May for spectacular waves of northward migrating warblers among the trees. Look for wood ducks in the swamps and in the ponds. Red-winged blackbirds and muskrats are two of the most commonly seen animals here. Green frogs compete with red-wings for the title of most vocal inhabitant.

Directions: By bus, take the S108 or the S113 from ferry terminal to Richmond Road and Rockland Avenue; walk one block along Rockland Avenue; turn right onto Nevada Avenue, and climb the hill to the pedestrian path leading to Visitor Center. By subway, take the IRT train from ferry terminal to New Dorp; walk up Altamount Street to High Rock Park. By car, from the Verrazano Narrows Bridge, take Staten Island Expressway (Interstate 287 West) to the Richmond Road exit; follow Richmond Road 0.75 miles; turn right again, onto Nevada Avenue; the main parking lot is on the left.

Ownership: City of New York Department of Parks and Recreation. Urban Park Rangers 1-800-201-PARK

Size: 90 acres   **Closest Town:** New Dorp

The black-throated green warbler is one of more than 30 species of wood warbler that pass through the city each spring to nesting grounds further north. It makes its summer home in northern coniferous and mixed forests, and winters in Central America.
ARTHUR MORRIS

NEW YORK CITY

63. CLAY PIT PONDS STATE PARK PRESERVE

Description: Named for a clay-mining operation that once thrived there, Clay Pit Ponds is today a mix of unique habitats including wetlands, fields, sandy barrens, spring-fed streams, and woodlands. New York City's first State Park Preserve, it is managed to retain its unique ecological systems and to provide educational and recreational opportunities for people of all ages. School, teacher, group, individual and family programming is offered year-round. Phone for a seasonal calendar of events and registration information. Visit the park headquarters building and then explore the two trails, one of which has an observation deck and bench. Sharrotts Pond also has an observation deck that is accessible to persons with disabilities.

Viewing Information: Each season offers different wildlife viewing experiences. Visit during spring and fall to witness the bird migrations. Summer offers opportunities to enjoy wading birds, waterfowl, frogs, and turtles in the ponds. Open water in the winter provides more waterfowl watching as well as chances to see birds of prey. Sharrotts Pond and Abraham's Pond offer excellent viewing opportunities. Experienced birders have recorded ospreys, eight species of hawks, and four species of owls. Guided walks provide the best chances to see birds of prey. Gray squirrels and cottontail rabbits are the most commonly viewed mammals. Watch in the ponds for snapping and spotted turtles and spring peepers. Look carefully along the trails for the Eastern box turtle and Fowler's toad. A real treat in the pine barrens area is a glimpse of a Northern fence lizard.

Directions: *By bus, from the ferry terminal, take the S74 bus to the stop at Arthur Kill Road and Sharrotts Road. Cross Arthur Kill Road and walk up Sharrotts Road. Take a left onto Carlin Street to its end. By car, take the Verrazano Bridge to Staten Island Expressway (Interstate 287 West) to the West Shore Expressway (Route 440 South) for approximately 6 miles to Exit 3, Bloomingdale Road. Turn left at the stop sign onto Bloomingdale Road. Drive for approximately 1 mile to Sharrotts Road and turn right. Approximately 0.75 miles on down Sharrotts, turn right onto Carlin to its end.*

Ownership: NYS Parks, Recreation and Historic Preservation 718-967-1976

Size: 260 acres   **Closest Town:** Staten Island

The best time to look for shy and elusive spotted turtles is in April, when they emerge from the water to sun themselves on logs or tussock sedges.
THOMAS D. LINDSAY

Description: Jamaica Bay Wildlife Refuge is one of the largest and best known wildlife viewing facilities in the New York City–Long Island area. Jamaica Bay is part of the Gateway National Recreation Area (other sites include Breezy Point, Staten Island, Sandy Hook), which covers a total of 26,000 acres. Jamaica Bay's diverse habitats include salt marsh, upland field, woods, several fresh and brackish water ponds, and an open expanse of bay and islands—all located within the city limits of New York City. More than 325 species of birds have been recorded here during the last 25 years. Several blinds along 5 miles of trails enhance viewing. "Gateway Visitors Companion", an excellent guide to the natural resources of the park, can be purchased at the Refuge Visitor Center.

Viewing Information: Each season provides different viewing opportunities: spring is best for warblers and songbirds, summer favors shorebirds, fall is best for migrating hawks and geese, and winter provides good hawk and owl viewing. Summer is also the best time to enjoy wading birds like egrets, herons, and the glossy ibis. Seeing the owls is always a special treat. Look for the saw-whet in evergreens and in the gardens. The refuge has a good population of barn owls, also found in the evergreens and gardens. Look for the short-eared owl during the winter in grassy fields. During June watch for the diamondback terrapin in salt marsh shallows and on trails.

Directions: *On Long Island, take the Belt Parkway to Cross Bay Boulevard South. Look for signs and the large visitor center and parking lot.*

Ownership: National Park Service 718-318-4340   **Size:** 9,155 acres

Closest Towns: Broad Channel and Howard Beach, Queens

One of the most abundant of the many species of small shorebirds affectionately called "peeps" by birders, semipalmated sandpipers feed on the tiny aquatic organisms exposed by retreating waves. Watch for them on the beach, running just inches away from the advancing and retreating surf. A. AND E. MORRIS

NEW YORK CITY

83

REGION SEVEN: COASTAL LOWLANDS

The coastal lowlands of Long Island are characterized by low topographic relief with a maximum elevation near 400 feet. Geologically, Long Island is the terminal moraine of a great ice sheet. It has the state's mildest climate, which is controlled by the surrounding heat-retaining Long Island Sound and the Atlantic Ocean. Due to its large and growing human population, the Coastal Lowlands lack some of the wildlife of upstate areas such as bear, beaver, otter, and bald eagle. On the other hand, Long Island's shores are the only places in New York from which people can see dolphins, seals, and whales. The shores are also the best places to see plovers, sandpipers, and gulls. Offshore, especially in winter along the barrier-island beaches, is where you are likely to see loons and sea ducks. Ospreys and waterfowl prefer sheltered bays and estuaries, of which Long Island has many. The vast pine barrens of the island's east-

ern end are austere in appearance but alive with many species of songbirds, reptiles, amphibians, wildflowers, and uncommon plants such as a dwarf form of the pitch pine. Eastern Long Island, with its extensive agricultural lands and colonial-style architecture, surrounded by water, can give the visitor the feeling of an ocean island—remote, beautiful, out of time's boundaries, and a good place to see wildlife.

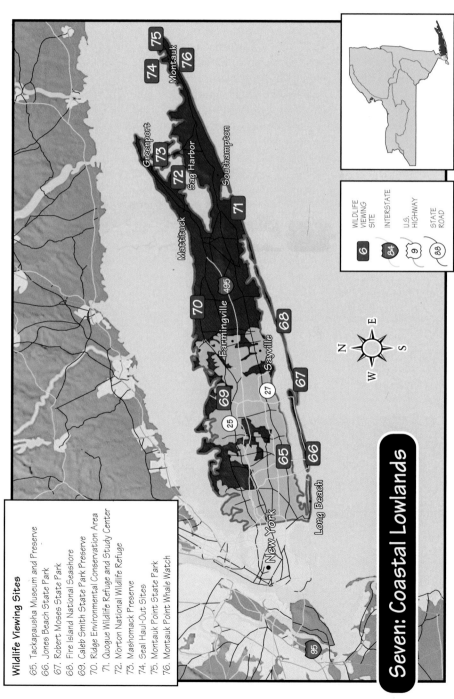

Wildlife Viewing Sites

65. Tackapausha Museum and Preserve
66. Jones Beach State Park
67. Robert Moses State Park
68. Fire Island National Seashore
69. Caleb Smith State Park Preserve
70. Ridge Environmental Conservation Area
71. Quogue Wildlife Refuge and Study Center
72. Morton National Wildlife Refuge
73. Mashomack Preserve
74. Seal Haul-Out Sites
75. Montauk Point State Park
76. Montauk Point Whale Watch

Seven: Coastal Lowlands

65. TACKAPAUSHA MUSEUM AND PRESERVE

Description: The museum houses many habitat and live animal displays interpreting Long Island's plant and animal life. Lying along Seaford Creek, the preserve's dominant habitat is wet, deciduous woods. Grassy fields, ponds, and freshwater marshes also occur here. Noteworthy is a stand of Atlantic white cedar, rare in Nassau County. The preserve is divided into three sections by two roads and each section has a separate entrance.

Viewing Information: Visit the museum first for an introduction to Long Island wildlife and for trail maps and a brochure. Of special interest is an exhibit of nocturnal animals living in a reversed day-night cycle. Access to the southern section of the preserve begins behind the bus parking area adjacent to the museum. Gray squirrels and Eastern chipmunks may be seen along the trail. Look for tracks of muskrats, raccoons, small rodents, and birds at the edge of the freshwater marsh. More than 170 species of birds have been seen in the preserve, which is surrounded by suburban development. Mallards, great blue herons, egrets, and glossy ibis feed on a small pond in the preserve's central section. Look for sunfish guarding their scooped out nests near the shore. You might see painted turtles sunning themselves at the water's edge, and listen for calling frogs.

Directions: The museum and preserve entrance are located on Washington Avenue north of Merrick Road in Seaford on Long Island's Nassau County. Merrick Road can be accessed from the east-west-running Sunrise Highway or the north-south-running Seaford-Oyster Bay Expressway.

Ownership: Nassau County Department of Recreation and Parks 516-571-7443

Size: 84 acres   **Closest Town:** Seaford

The chipmunk is an appealing little rodent with bulging food pouches, common in woodlands and cultivated land throughout the east. They form an important part of the diet of many predators, from weasels to hawks. They hibernate during the winter on a bed of cached food that they awaken from time to time to eat. TOM VEZO

66. JONES BEACH STATE PARK

Description: One of the state's largest and most heavily used parks, with seven to eight million visitors annually, Jones Beach is best known for its bathing beach. However, its seashore, dunes, and protected marshes make Jones Beach a premier wildlife viewing site, as well. While its diverse habitats encourage all types of viewing, visitors often choose to focus on the beach and dune habitats.

Viewing Information: Since Jones Beach extends for 6.5 miles along the seashore, and since some of the best wildlife watching is in the spring and fall, many wildlife viewing sites are free from bathers. Out beyond the surf in the Atlantic look for eider, oldsquaw, and scoters. More than 30 species of shorebirds visit Jones Beach's beaches and tidal flats. Most common are greater and lesser yellowlegs, willets, spotted sandpipers, sanderlings, semipalmated, western, and least sandpipers, and short-billed dowitcher. Many species of gulls and eight species of terns can be seen at one time or another throughout the year. Black skimmers put on quite a show, fishing while flying with their lower bill just beneath the water surface. Two bitterns, several herons, egrets, and night herons grace the marshlands. Brant feed both in the water and out on the lawns. Five plovers, including the killdeer, feed at Jones Beach. A protected piping plover breeding area can be viewed from a safe distance. Watch for hawks, especially kestrels and peregrine falcons, migrating along the beach in the spring and fall. Most at home throughout the year is the Northern harrier, which hunts slow and low over the marsh. Snowy owls can be seen in the west end from December to March. Birds aren't the only wildlife. Watch for deer and other mammals among the dunes.

Directions: *On Long Island, take the Meadowbrook Parkway South or Wantagh Parkway South to its end.*

Ownership: NYS Parks, Recreation and Historic Preservation 516-785-1600

Size: 2,400 acres   **Closest Town:** Wantagh

Its large size and blackish mantle make the great black-backed among the easiest gulls to identify. It is fond of high soaring and wheeling. In summer it preys upon the eggs and young of ducks, cormorants, terns, and even other gulls.

TOM VEZO

COASTAL LOWLANDS

67. ROBERT MOSES STATE PARK

Description: Located on the western end of Long Island's Fire Island barrier beach, Robert Moses State Park provides visitors with easy access to 5 miles of shoreline and dune wildlife viewing. During the summer, many thousands of beach-goers visit for picnicking, fishing, swimming, surfing, and sunbathing, and to use the pitch-putt golf course. Wildlife viewing is excellent throughout the year. During the summer, seek wildlife in areas away from the bathing beaches.

Viewing Information: Park in Parking Field 2 and walk on the beach to the west. From Parking Field 5, walk to the vehicle turnaround loop for viewing to the east. In April and May, stop off on the way to or from Robert Moses at Captree State Park to see the herring gulls nesting right beside the parking lots. At Robert Moses, watch for Northern harriers with their distinctive white rump patches soaring low over the ground in search of rodents. Watch for double-crested cormorants all year and great cormorants in winter. You might see green and great blue herons, great and snowy egrets, and the glossy ibis feeding in the emergent vegetation in the Fire Island Inlet shallows. They often rest and roost in trees. Look carefully at the Canada geese; smaller brant, with a less distinct neck patch, are also seen here. Mallard, black duck, and red-breasted merganser are the three most abundant of the nearly two dozen duck species. Five species of plover, from the killdeer to the federally-listed threatened piping plover, are beach dwellers. The sanderling is the most abundant of the many sandpipers. Watch for oystercatchers with their large red-orange bills designed to pry mollusk shells open. From September to mid-October, watch the raptor migration along beaches and dunes. Also watch for monarch butterflies gathering to await northerly winds to carry them south along the coast to Mexico. Many species of wood warblers and other songbirds migrate through during spring and fall, but one, the yellow-rumped warbler, overwinters in bayberry thickets eating the waxy fruit. These thickets also attract deer.

Directions: *On mid-Long Island in Suffolk County, take the Sagtikos State Parkway south to the Robert Moses Causeway, which crosses Great South Bay. You will come first to Captree Island and then, continuing on the Causeway, to Robert Moses State Park.*

Ownership: NYS Parks, Recreation and Historic Preservation 516-669-0449

Size: 858 acres   **Closest Town:** Babylon

Osprey are now breeding on Long Island, but New York's fish hawk was once decimated by the pesticide DDT. Since DDT was banned in 1971, osprey numbers have increased dramatically, and in 1983 the species was removed from the endangered species list.

Description: Fire Island National Seashore's 22 miles of barrier beach annually provides millions of visitors quality recreational experiences. In addition to the interpretive visitor centers and wildlife viewing, swimming, camping, food service, and marinas for boaters are available. Besides the more easily accessed sites described here, private boats or passenger ferries enable visits to Sailors Haven from Sayville and Watch Hill from Patchogue. At Smith Point, a visitor center with exhibits and interpretive programs is open weekends during the summer. A self-guided, boardwalk nature-trail loop provides access from the parking lot to the ocean beach. At the William Floyd Estate, the grounds are open daily for hiking and wildlife viewing.

Viewing Information: The booklet that interprets Smith Point's self-guided trail provides an interesting description of the characteristic features of a barrier beach and the plants and animals that make their home here. Off shore, watch for dolphins and pilot whales. On the beach, the sanderling is the most common of the sandpipers. Visitors can easily identify all four of the common gull species here: ring-billed, herring, laughing, and great black-backed. The piping plover, federally listed as threatened, can occasionally be seen. Whelks, clams, blue crabs, and jellyfish occur on the beach and bayshore. Red foxes, gray catbirds, rufous-sided towhees, and Fowler's toads inhabit the swales and thickets. White-tailed deer and cottontail rabbits are here, too. Not located on Fire Island, the William Floyd Estate is quite different from the barrier island. Fields, woods, and ponds attract a variety of wildlife. A salt marsh bordering Moriches Bay is especially interesting.

Directions: *Smith Point and William Floyd Estate are located on the south shore of Long Island's Suffolk County. Smith Point: Take the William Floyd Parkway South across Smith Point Bridge to the pay parking lot at the adjacent Smith Point County Park. William Floyd Estate: Take the William Floyd Parkway to Neighborhood Road's eastern end. Turn left onto Park Drive and go four blocks to the entrance.*

Ownership: National Park Service, U.S. Department of the Interior 516-289-4810

Size: 22 miles of barrier beach   **Closest Towns:** Mastic and Shirley

The snowy owl often wanders south in winter to feed on rodents and sea birds on our coastal dunes. White feathers help it disappear into its snowy home environment, and its feathered legs help retain body heat. TOM VEZO

COASTAL LOWLANDS

69. CALEB SMITH STATE PARK PRESERVE

Description: Owned by the same family for more than 200 years, the preserve is named for the original resident of the large home that today serves as the nature museum. A variety of aquatic and terrestrial habitats provide an oasis for wildlife surrounded by suburban development.

Viewing Information: Two self-guided nature trails enable visitors to explore the preserve and become familiar with its plants and animals and their relationships to each other. A permit to use the trails may be obtained in the museum building, which houses extensive interpretive exhibits and live and preserved animals. Some of the best wildlife viewing is on Willow Pond, located near the parking area and museum. Mute swan, Canada goose, mallard, wood duck, great blue heron, belted kingfisher and osprey all breed in the preserve and are frequently seen here. Gadwall, northern shoveler, and ring-necked duck overwinter. Chipmunk, gray, and even southern flying squirrels inhabit the forest. Two stations along the Self-guided Nature Trail provide good winter wildlife viewing: the bird-feeding area with a blind and the planting fields where food crops attract many birds and mammals.

Directions: The preserve is 47 miles east of New York City on Long Island in Suffolk County. Take either the Long Island Expressway (Interstate 495), Northern State Parkway or Southern State Parkway (East) to the Sunken Meadow State Parkway (North) to Exit SM3-East and then take Jericho Turnpike East to the preserve entrance.

Ownership: NYS Parks, Recreation and Historic Preservation 516-265-1054

Size: 543 acres   **Closest Town:** Smithtown

The gadwall normally occurs in small flocks and seldom seems abundant. It is noteworthy, though, in having the widest range of any duck in the world. Shallow streams, ponds, and lakes are favorite haunts. TOM VEZO

70. RIDGE ENVIRONMENTAL CONSERVATION AREA

Description: This conservation area is actively managed to provide many types of wildlife habitat. A varied mowing schedule insures that grasslands, early shrub successional stages, thickets, and young forest stands are always present. A freshwater pond and a mature oak–pine forest are more permanent features. This management provides food, water, shelter, and nesting sites for many wildlife species.

Viewing Information: Owned by New York State since 1914, the site was originally a ring-necked pheasant and bobwhite quail game farm. Both birds can be seen here, but are no longer raised on site. Two trails, one a 1.5-mile loop and the other 2.5 miles, lead visitors through all of the area's habitats. The Randall Pond Nature Trail booklet keyed to numbered stations interprets the habitats and the plants and animals each support. You might see white-tailed deer, cottontail rabbits and box turtles anywhere along the trail. Other animals are more site specific: Meadowlarks and field and grasshopper sparrows inhabit grassy areas. Catbirds, robins, and cedar waxwings eat berries that grow in thickets. Belted kingfishers, spotted sandpipers, great blue herons, and several ducks are at home at Randall Pond. Look in the shallow water near shore for male pumpkinseed sunfish guarding their circular nests. In the forest, gray squirrels are active by day and flying squirrels begin their long glides at dusk.

Directions: *In Suffolk County on Long Island, take the Long Island Expressway (Interstate 495) to Exit 68. Take the William Floyd Parkway North to Route 25 West 0.25 mile to Randall Road. Turn right onto Randall Road and go 500 feet to the entrance on the left.*

Ownership: NYS Department of Environmental Conservation 516-444-0305

Size: 200 acres   **Closest Town:** Ridge

Common in mature woodlands, the spectacular scarlet tanager spends most of its time in the treetops where it feeds on leaf-eating insects. Let its hoarse robin-like song help you spot it.
TOM VEZO

71. QUOGUE WILDLIFE REFUGE AND STUDY CENTER

Description: Quogue's trails and boardwalks, through pine barrens and acid bog, past three freshwater ponds and fresh and brackish swamps, provide some of the best wildlife viewing on eastern Long Island. The nature center interprets the outdoor habitats and animals.

Viewing Information: Spring is the best time to visit for pine barrens wildflowers and the songbird migration. The ponds support large numbers of mallards, black ducks, and Canada geese. Watch for great blue heron along the edges. By wearing polarizing sunglasses on the bridge, it is possible to look down into the water for warm-water fish including bass, sunfish, yellow perch, catfish, pickerel, and eel. Pick up a trail guide booklet at the Nature Center and use it to follow the 20-station marked trail.

Directions: *Near the south shore of eastern Long Island, from Route 27, take Exit 64 to Route 104 South to Old Country Road West to the refuge.*

Ownership: NYS Department of Environmental Conservation 516-653-4771

Size: 300 acres   **Closest Town:** Quogue

72. MORTON NATIONAL WILDLIFE REFUGE

Description: Morton is located on eastern Long Island's south fork overlooking Peconic Bay to the west and Noyack Bay to the east. The wooded bluffs of Jessups Neck, a 1.75-mile-long sandy, gravel, rocky-beached peninsula separates the two bays. The remainder of this exceptional refuge is upland forest, brackish and freshwater ponds, saltmarsh, a lagoon, and fields.

Viewing Information: The refuge is managed to protect this unique natural area for migratory birds while other wildlife benefit as well: deer, fox, squirrel, cottontail, woodchuck, muskrat, and reptiles. Since endangered and threatened species such as piping plover, least tern, roseate tern, and osprey use the refuge for nesting, brood rearing, feeding, and resting, public access to the peninsula is closed during the breeding season—April through August. A wheelchair-accessible interpretive kiosk and restrooms are located at the headquarters area.

Directions: *From Route 27, on eastern Long Island, turn north at Exit 8 onto North Sea Road (Route 38), to North Sea/Noyack Roads. Continue on to Noyack Road (Route 38). The refuge is 5 miles on the left.*

Ownership: Department of the Interior, U.S. Fish and Wildlife Service 516-286-0485. Inquire about other sites in the Long Island National Wildlife Refuge Complex: Target Rock NWR, Wertheim NWR.

Size: 187 acres   **Closest Town:** Sag Harbor

Description: Covering a third of Shelter Island, the preserve was acquired by The Nature Conservancy to preserve this nearly pristine peninsula and to protect one of the most dense populations of breeding osprey on the east coast. With 10 miles of coastline, Mashomack is an area of extraordinary scenic beauty. A visitor center with interesting exhibits is staffed by volunteers daily during the summer and on weekends the rest of the year.

Viewing Information: Four loop trails ranging from 1.5 to 11 miles enable visitors to explore much of the preserve. For visitors wanting a shorter walk, an accessible Braille trail (less than 0.1 mile in length) passes the native plant garden, a woodland, and a freshwater kettle. Mashomack is best known for its bird life. Nearly 200 species have been recorded here; about 75 nest on the preserve. Some commonly seen wading birds include great blue herons, great and snowy egrets, green herons and black-crowned night herons. Oldsquaw and white-winged scoter are two sea ducks common both fall and winter. The strikingly marked ruddy turnstone is the most abundant of the sandpipers. White-tailed deer, gray squirrels, eastern chipmunks, and raccoons live among the trees and shrubs here.

Directions: Located at the eastern end of Long Island, 90 miles from New York City, Shelter Island is accessible either on the North Ferry from Greenport or the South Ferry from North Haven. From the north, follow Route 114 three miles south to the entrance. From the south, the preserve is 1 mile north on Route 114.

Ownership: The Nature Conservancy 516-749-1001

Size: 2,039 acres **Closest Town:** Shelter Island

Osprey nest wherever extensive bodies of clear water and elevated nest sites exist. Their food is exclusively fish, which they spot from a height of from 30 to 100 feet. Half closing their wings, they plunge into the water, seizing their prey with their talons. They then rise quickly, shake off the water, and set out for their nest. TOM VEZO

COASTAL LOWLANDS

74. SEAL HAUL-OUT SITES

Description: Fourteen sites are identified on Long and Staten islands: Hungry Point; East, Middle, and West Clump on Fishers Island; South Beach on Great Gull Island; Eastern Point on Plum Island; Rock Reef outside the jetty at Sag Harbor; sand spits on the southern end of Gardiners Island; Blackfish Rock Cove in Montauk Point State Park, Montauk; Shinnecock Inlet and bars north of Shinnecock Inlet; Dredge Spoil Island north of Moriches Inlet (visible from Cupsogue Beach County Park); Democrat Point on Fire Island; Deep Creek Meadow, Cow Islands; Jones Bay Sloop Channel (accessible by boat from Freeport and Town of Hempstead); Silver Point Park, Atlantic Beach and Hicks Beach in Reynolds Channel; Grassy Hassock Channel Islands on the north side, near Kennedy Airport; Rockaway Inlet Park, north side, Rockaway; and Cookes Point outside Great Kills Harbor on Staten Island.

Viewing Information: Seals haul out on land to rest, dry out, and condition their coats. This is a daily activity except during foul weather (meaning extreme windchill or very rough seas). From the beginning of November to the beginning of June, harbor and gray seals haul out at low tide at the sites named above. In the summer months, however, increased human activity near haul out sites forces seals to relocate to inaccessible, non-viewable haul outs. SEAL WATCHING ETIQUETTE: To optimize your enjoyment and that of others while respecting the well-being of the seals, please do not approach closer than 100 yards. Use binoculars or spotting scopes to see the animals more closely. Wear dark clothing to reduce the accentuation of your movement, move slowly and smoothly, and speak in a quiet voice.

Directions: *See map*

Ownership: Various

Size: Not applicable   **Closest Town:** See map

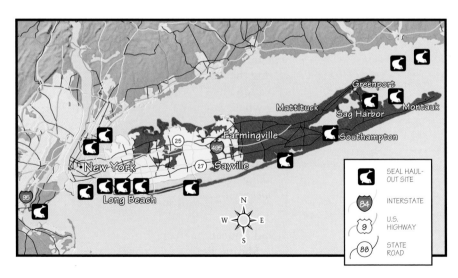

75. MONTAUK POINT STATE PARK

Description: With its picturesque lighthouse on the bluff as a focal point, Montauk Point provides excellent year-round, day-use wildlife viewing.

Viewing Information: The varied upland habitats are home to white-tailed deer, raccoons, red fox, weasels, and cottontail rabbits. A good variety of song-birds, dominated by the mockingbird, nest here. Watch for box turtles along the trail and for whales swimming offshore. In winter, harbor seals can be conveniently seen from viewing blinds. Also during the winter watch for harlequin ducks, surf and black scoters, red-breasted mergansers, and razorbills in the surf.

Directions: *Take the Long Island Expressway (Interstate 495) to Exit 70 South to Sunrise Highway (Route 27) East to the end of Long Island.*

Ownership: NYS Parks, Recreation and Historic Preservation 516-668-3781

Size: 724 acres   **Closest Town:** Montauk

76. MONTAUK POINT WHALE WATCH

Description: See the world's largest mammals aboard the Sunbeam Express on an interpreted four- to seven-hour cruise. The boat travels 12 to 17 miles southeast out of Montauk Point to where the animals congregate. An on-board naturalist describes the whales and their behaviors. Cruises are conducted Wednesdays through Sundays, 10 A.M. to 4 P.M. from May 15 to September 15.

Viewing Information: From this whale-watching boat, seven species of whale and three species of dolphin can be seen during the spring and summer months: finback, hump-backed, sperm, right, pilot, and minke whales; white-sided, common, and bottle-nosed dolphins. Visitors might see leatherback sea turtles, ocean sunfish, and basking shark. Whale watches also provide excellent opportunities to see pelagic birds. Other fish you might see are hammerhead shark and bluefin tuna. Using the same docks, the Riverhead Foundation for Marine Research and Preservation and Cornell Cooperative Extension join with the Viking Fleet in offering whale watch and ocean education cruises.

Directions: *Take the Long Island Expressway (Interstate 495) to the end, Exit 73, labeled Route 58 Riverhead. Continue east through Riverhead approximately 5 miles to Route 25 and the intersection of Route 105. Continue east on Route 25 approximately 25 miles to the blinking light at the T intersection in Montauk. Turn left towards the water. Prestons Dock is 50 yards away on the left. Municipal parking is on the right.*

Ownership: Coastal Research and Education Society of Long Island 516-287-8223. Riverhead Foundation for Marine Research and Preservation 516-369-9840

Size: N/A   **Closest Town:** Montauk

COASTAL LOWLANDS

FRANKLIN MOUNTAIN HAWK WATCH

Note: This additional site belongs in Region Two, Appalachian Plateau.

Description: This 100-acre Audubon sanctuary offers a marsh, abandoned pastures, mixed forest, and the mountain itself with a panoramic view to the north over Oneonta and the Susquehanna Valley.

Viewing Information: Although the sanctuary offers songbird and other wildlife viewing throughout the year, Franklin Mountain is visited most often from mid-September through November during the height of the eagle and hawk migration. Experienced bundled-up birders bring spotting scopes and binoculars following a cold front to see birds soaring on northwest or north winds. Golden and bald eagles are the raptors most frequently sought, but turkey vultures and many other hawks are also counted. As many as 1,231 red-tailed hawks have been seen in a single day. A record 27 golden eagles have been spotted in a day. Knowledgeable birders are often on hand during the peak season to answer questions and help with identification.

Directions: From Interstate 88 in the foothills of the Catskills, take Exit 15. Turn south onto Route 28. At first stoplight, turn right and go to third stoplight (0.7 mile). Turn left and immediately left again at T intersection onto South Side Drive. Go 0.8 mile and turn right onto Swart Hollow Road. Go 1.5 miles and make sharp right onto Grange Hall Road. After 0.2 mile, turn left into first driveway and park along the side. Walk to barn. Turn left and follow path up hill 100 yards. The site has a raised mound, benches and an information kiosk.

Ownership: Delaware-Otsego Audubon Society 607-432-3841

Size: 100 acres   **Closest Town:** Oneonta